JUSTIN STEELE

IDAN RAVIN is a basketball trainer who works with many of the world's top players. He splits his time between suburban Maryland and New York City.

THE HOOPS WHISPERER

ON THE COURT AND INSIDE THE HEADS OF
BASKETBALL'S BEST PLAYERS

IDAN RAVIN

AVERY
an imprint of Penguin Random House
New York

an imprint of Penguin Random House LLC
375 Hudson Street
New York, New York 10014

First trade paperback edition, May 2015
Previously published in hardcover by Gotham Books
Copyright © 2014 by Idan Ravin

Most Avery books are available at special quantity discounts for bulk purchase for sales promotions, premiums, fund-raising, and educational needs. Special books or book excerpts also can be created to fit specific needs. For details, write SpecialMarkets @penguinrandomhouse.com.

The Library of Congress has catalogued the hardcover edition as follows:

Ravin, Idan.
The hoops whisperer : on the court and inside the heads of basketball's best players / Idan Ravin.
p.   cm.
ISBN 978-1-59240-891-7
1. Basketball—Training.   2. Basketball—Psychological aspects.   3. Basketball players—United States.   4. Athletes—Life-skills guides.   5. Success.
6. Ravin, Idan.   I. Title.
GV885.35.R38   2014   2013046340
796.323—dc23

ISBN 978-1-59240-937-2 (paperback)

Printed in the United States of America
3   5   7   9   10   8   6   4   2

Book design by Elke Sigal

*Penguin is committed to publishing works of quality and integrity.
In that spirit, we are proud to offer this book to our readers;
however, the story, the experiences, and the words
are the author's alone.*

For Mom

Mairav · **MY FIRST TEAM** · Aynat

Dad

CONTENTS

It is not proper to be ashamed of any game. This is no child's play. It is wrong for adults to say—and for the more intelligent of the children to repeat after them, "Such a big boy and he plays like a baby; such a big girl and she still plays with dolls." What matters is not what one plays with, but rather how and what one thinks and feels while playing. One can play wisely with a doll or play childishly and foolishly at chess. One can play with great interest and imagination at being a policeman, making a train, being a hunter or an Indian, and one can read books without any thought or interest.

—JANUSZ KORCZAK, "'RULES OF LIFE,'
A CHILDHOOD OF DIGNITY"

INTRODUCTION

Becoming Lamar Mundane

the greatest life becomes the one u never imagined
#blessed

In the late 1980s, a television commercial aired for a new line of Reebok high-tops. The black-and-white ad began with several teenagers huddled together on the stoop of a brownstone, nodding their heads as an older man shared the story of a playground legend named Lamar Mundane. He described watching Lamar Mundane effortlessly release his jump shot from as far as fifty feet away, over the outstretched arms of defenders, with the onlookers shouting, "Money," as the ball kissed the clouds before falling through the net.

I wanted to wear those high-tops. I wanted to do the things Lamar Mundane had done. I wanted to live on a city block within walking distance of a playground with a basketball court surrounded by a chain-link fence so an audience could witness my game. I wanted to take on the city's best players. I wanted folks to talk about my game with the same reverence. I also wanted to trade places with those boys on the stoop, even for just a moment, so I could hear the tales of the playground legends.

A few years ago, I received a call from Carmelo Anthony's agent at the time asking if I could assist on a commercial that Nike's Jordan Brand was scheduled to shoot with Melo as part of the launch of his new signature shoe. Melo and I had worked together since he'd left Syracuse after his freshman year in 2003. The call from his agent surprised me, because generally I dealt directly with the players with regards to scheduling, training, billing, etc. Most agents were proprietary about their clients and felt uncomfortable knowing that someone had burrowed his way into their client's circle without the agent's blessing. In any event, Melo was "my guy," as players I've worked with would say, and I would have flown to Timbuktu if he'd asked, even with only thirty minutes' notice and just the clothes on my back. I was available and I suggested the production company contact me to coordinate logistics.

"You won't be getting paid for this," his agent reminded me.

Too bad we weren't on Skype so he could see me smile. Money was never my motivator. I loved what I did. Whatever came with it was just gravy.

I flew to Los Angeles several days later. I arrived on set a day early to meet with Jesse, the ad agency's creative director on the account, and Brian, the director. They didn't seem overly excited; they'd researched and prepared their treatment weeks earlier, and they probably thought I'd suggest things they had already seen, posted on YouTube by other trainers.

I'd recently come up with a few new drills for Melo involving tennis balls, hand gestures, cones, and multiple basketballs, and I thought these would resonate on camera. Their energy changed once I demonstrated the scope and complexity of Melo's training.

Brian positioned his hands in the shape of a camera lens to visualize how to frame and shoot each drill, while Jesse asked me to explain the drill and its purpose.

"Yes. Very cool! This is going to be great! I love it! You're intense!" they said, maybe not in that order.

I didn't tell them that I might have to audible from the intended outline, depending on what I felt from Melo once he stepped out of his trailer. You can't be wedded to a script when working with superstars. Sensitivity to their rhythms is important. If I sensed reluctance, I would pull back. If I sensed excitement, I would push forward. If I sensed indifference, I'd play it by ear.

The following day Melo arrived in the early afternoon on a flight from Asia. He had spent the last several weeks representing the United States in the world championships in Japan. I assumed he would be exhausted from all the travel, practices, games, and off-court commitments required when you represent your country.

"Keep the takes to a minimum. He doesn't have much gas left in the tank," I told Brian.

Efficiency was paramount, not only for Melo, but also for the ad agency and production company under orders to deliver top content to their shoe company client.

Our first scene involved Melo shooting jump shots from beyond the NBA arc. The second scene showed Melo catching a tennis ball with one hand while dribbling with the other and moving in different directions based on my commands. The drill refined his ball control because it overloaded his senses to simulate the intense distractions he faces under game conditions: long and active defenders, screaming fans, teammates in motion, coaches calling out plays, clocks ticking down, referees circling, and television crews hoping to capture great footage.

The third scene showcased his ability to anticipate defensive pressure, identify passing opportunities, and handle the ball all at once. I stood almost directly behind him, just slightly off-center. Keeping his back to me, he dribbled while I flashed different numbers with my fingers; relying only on his peripheral vision, he had to call out the number of fingers I signaled without losing the dribble. This went on for a minute, and I switched between his right and left side every few seconds.

The fourth scene highlighted Melo's agility and explosiveness. Melo caught the ball near the foul line with his back to the basket. I stood behind him, pushing a big rectangular pad against his back to mimic the defensive pressure he can expect when he plays. He paused once he caught the ball to feel the contact from the pad, then rotated his left pivot foot inward and exploded to the basket, jumping off both feet for a monstrous two-handed dunk.

The fifth scene emphasized his efficiency and speed as Melo sprinted from baseline to baseline for a layup while taking just three dribbles, pushing the ball forward, and running after it. Brian wanted some additional takes, and the day of shooting was getting long. Melo never complained, but I noticed his stern look substituting for his usual warm smile.

The last scene demonstrated Melo's lateral mobility as he took his defensive stance and quickly slid his feet from side to side to get to the passes I threw to his left and his right. As soon as Brian issued a thumbs-up, Melo pushed open the gym doors, tossed his headband to the floor, walked down the hill toward his trailer past the many fans stationed outside the gym, and collapsed on the couch in his trailer.

The ad agency called a few weeks later. My voice was muffled during one of the scenes, so they needed to rerecord. When I arrived at the editors' offices, they handed me a script and headphones as they escorted me to a soundproof booth, then played the scene on a monitor in front of me. The script did not jibe with anything I would say to Melo, so I improvised. Afterward, we sat in another office, where they played the rough edits of the commercial.

Over the course of the next sixty seconds I felt disbelief, awe, gratitude, humility, relief, joy, and hope. I had never seen myself on television or even on video. When I played ball in high school, neither our coaches nor my parents ever recorded our games or practices. I had been working with some of the NBA's best players for a number of years, but always deep in the shadows, in closed gyms and private circumstance, where the things I taught could be learned most effectively. But now a future audience of millions would see me, hear my voice, and view the unique relationship of trust I had built with Melo.

I privately wondered what the ad agency, the production company, the shoe company, and the athletes I trained would think if they knew my secrets. What if they discovered I didn't have a traditional basketball background, that I struggled for so long, that I loved the game more than I could ever eloquently express, that I'd chased an orange leather ball for decades not knowing where it would take me, that I'd converted my lifelong romance into something my landlord could rely on each month, that I operated under a cloak of anonymity for as long as I could remember, that I didn't know whether to cry or scream with joy at the moment?

Several weeks later I was running on a treadmill and saw the commercial on the television above me. I hit the stop button while in full stride, straddled the treadmill, and watched. I was not alone, but I didn't bother to wipe away the tears that pooled around my eyes and trickled down my cheeks. I never could have imagined this life.

Once upon a time I was a teenager inspired by a commercial, and now, years later, I had become the teenager on the stoop, the man narrating the story of a playground legend, and had even traded places with the legendary Lamar Mundane.

CHAPTER ONE

THE KING AND PI

4 letters can connect a universe
#love #ball #game

During the summer of 2008, I was in New Orleans for several days working with Chris Paul, who was then playing for the Hornets. In just his third pro season, barely twenty-three years old, he was already a first-team All-NBA guard. We were in NOLA so he could attend the annual Essence Music Festival, the largest event celebrating African-American culture and music in the United States.

Our mornings started early with a thirty-minute drive from Canal Street to the gym we were using, stopping along the way at a fast-food drive-thru, where we found the best of the worst breakfast options before our workout. Afterward, he showered and changed uniforms, going from NBA All-Star to fashionable golfer before meeting his brother, CJ, at the golf course to play a round or even two before getting ready for the night's festival events. On one of our days in the Big Easy, he told me we'd be starting late the next day. Unusual, I thought, since Chris prefers to race the sun so he can get the most out of his day. He didn't give a reason, and I didn't ask for one.

I found out why the next day. "Bron's comin' to work out with us this morning," he mentioned when we arrived at the gym.

"Cool." What else could I say?

I first learned of LeBron James years earlier when I read about a sophomore from Ohio who dominated a USA Basketball tryout for high school players in Colorado Springs. The report called him the best player in America, even as a tenth grader. Such mythic descriptions of a sixteen-year-old, an age when puberty creates noticeable physical distinctions among high school players, led me to Fairleigh Dickinson University to see him play at the famed Adidas ABCD Camp. He ran faster, jumped higher, shot farther, dunked harder, and passed better than anyone I had ever seen at that age. Had someone told me he played in the NBA, I would have believed it up until the moment when I saw his youth reflected in his facial features.

Now he was a twenty-three-year-old already being considered among the all-time greats. And today I was going to get the closest possible look at his incredible physical presence.

His massive frame dwarfed the friends and associates who came along with him to the gym. He seemed taller than the 6-8 listed in the media guide, probably because his heels rarely touched the ground when he walked; he propelled himself forward on the balls of his feet while rotating his feet externally with each step, akin to the gait of a ballerina in toe shoes. I assumed he weighed more than 250 pounds, but his bulk was masked by his even proportions and amazing balance of lean muscle, impossibly low body fat, and herculean strength. Standing near him reminded me of resting beside a mature oak tree on a family trip to Yosemite.

I knew that even my casual introduction that morning from his best friend Chris wouldn't earn me LeBron's attention, respect, or effort, all of which would be necessary for the session to be worthwhile for either of us. If I wanted to make any kind of impression, I'd have to proceed with authority and care.

Other than short hellos, I said nothing more to him, his manager, or the rest of his friends sitting along the bleachers. Dressed in blue Nike shorts, white tee, and his signature basketball shoe, he shot the ball effortlessly from afar as we prepared to start. Tone and privacy matter a lot to me, so I hoped having his guests at the gym wouldn't affect the intensity of our session or his willingness to try new things. With each accomplishment, superstars like LeBron step closer to the clouds and farther from the ground, which means when they fail at anything even briefly, they seem to tumble harder and faster; being aware of the consequences can make someone less experimental and daring. I respect and understand why superstars insulate themselves with grade-school friends they've always trusted. Having their childhoods represented lets them subconsciously create normalcy in their already abnormal lives.

But the gym has to be a place of humility. It's our classroom. If you come in there with ego, you won't learn. If you come in there with stardom on your shoulder, you'll be afraid to make a mistake. If you come in there carrying too much pride, you won't acknowledge your weaknesses and work on them. That's why I prefer to keep the gym closed to visitors; I want your focus and your intensity, with no thought about how anything looks or what anyone else thinks.

"Let's get started, fellas," I hollered as I tossed the basketballs they'd been casually shooting toward the baseline. I pulled Chris aside to instruct him on the first drill. I spoke loud enough for the others to hear me, but not enough to make it seem that I was talking to anyone other than Chris. Passive disregard, I called it. Fame feeds on attention, and that was something I couldn't immediately give LeBron without compromising me or my message.

Chris went first, a warm-up of five layups: a sprint from each baseline corner, from the sidelines at the foul line extended, and from half-court down the lane to the basket. I didn't look at LeBron until he took his turn and I didn't intend to offer any additional instruction, gauging his focus by how well he'd studied Chris and Portland Trail Blazers guard Jarrett Jack, who went before him. He started out by sprinting toward the basket, but I swiped the ball from out of his hands and intentionally struck his forearm. The ball rolled out of bounds.

"They take once you drop," I said, demonstrating how he had just lowered the ball below his midsection.

He returned to his starting position, then dashed toward the basket, keeping the ball high as I tried to swipe down on it on each of his five attempts. I nodded as he looked back at me after.

Our session progressed in intensity and soon involved sets of multiple twenty-two-foot jump shots taken from seven places around the three-point arc and incorporating a dart to half-court. First we shot off the catch, but as fatigue set in, the drill evolved into covering as much ground as possible with one long dribble angled at forty-five degrees to simulate exploding past a defender. Chris again went first and converted most of his shots. We'd done this drill in many gyms over the last few years, so he understood the mechanics and spacing. Experience taught him to keep a strong and consistent pace because of the lung capacity the drill demanded. Jarrett Jack and two of LeBron's high school teammates who were also working out were bent over and tugging on their shorts to keep themselves upright after their turn.

LeBron went next but first asked about the angle of the initial dribble and where to hold the ball when he received the pass.

"Away from your chest so you can avoid the closeout," I quickly explained, keeping the conversation limited and deliberately vague.

He stood upright when I passed him the ball.

"Too high," I yelled while holding my hand horizontally to reinforce the importance of staying low.

He nodded, then tossed the ball to me; I passed it back to him like a hot potato. He caught it in a crouched position, chest up, knees bent, and weight forward, balanced on the balls of his feet. Perfect.

I tried to calculate his stride length as I watched him cover the court in as few steps as I'd ever seen. *Nine to ten feet*, I thought. The world had never seen such athleticism bottled in this size and shape. LeBron could sprint barefoot on the hardwood floors in my folks' home without making enough noise to wake my pop from a nap on the couch. He produced the power of a race car, yet struck the ground with incredible grace.

"You'll be aight," Chris said as he nudged LeBron, who was breathing heavily immediately after his set.

Soon we transitioned to stationary ball-handling, which required each player to generate even more force on the ball while manipulating it at different angles with the wrist and hand— like getting a golf ball to slice, hook, fade, or draw. The players stood along the baseline. LeBron now had my full attention. His eyes would trail the ball, which caused his head and torso to slump forward. I tapped his chin gently and then again with more force, eventually putting my forearm under his chin to raise his head upward. The sensation would reinforce the lesson and help him recall it until it became natural to him.

At the end of the session I went over to where an exhausted LeBron sat on the floor.

"You are far and away the most talented player in the league, way more talented than Kobe," I told him. "But you don't even have a go-to move in isolation, you can't handle the ball that well, and you can't shoot that well yet either. Think about that."

He couldn't disagree with the assessment after the workout we'd just finished, spotlighting some of these exact flaws.

"I'm not here to hurt your feelings," I added. "I'm trying to help you get better. You're a thirty, eight, and eight guy [points, rebounds, assists], and there's so much yet to do. That's *exciting*."

I left him alone after that. I did overhear him say to Chris, "That's why you're the best point guard in the world."

Afterward, a security detail escorted our convoy of sport utility vehicles to help expedite our return to the Ritz-Carlton on Canal Street. We unloaded our gear and headed to a small banquet room for breakfast. I sat with Jarrett Jack and Rudy Gay, who at the time played for the Memphis Grizzlies, as we waited for the catering staff to finalize the buffet. I watched Bron, Chris, and their mutual friends joke at their table, and I admired their close friendships. Over a generous serving of New Orleans brunch, Bron came over to thank me for the workout. It was my pleasure, I answered. I said, "Eighty percent of you would still be better than ninety-nine percent of the league."

"You right," he said.

But just imagine, I thought, *what 99 percent of you would be like. Isn't that intriguing? Don't you want to know?*

With all that, though, I didn't say a word about getting together again. I didn't ask for his number or suggest we schedule another session. I didn't have his contact information, and I didn't need it. I figured if he wanted to get in touch with me, he'd find a way to do it.

It's not that I get a kick out of playing hard to get. But superstars live in a world of their own, built around them and for them. They dictate everything. The only chance I had of helping LeBron get better was by letting him know that I wasn't looking to be his friend or his fan; he had enough of those already. I just wanted to do the work, not dance at the party.

Dealing with such high-powered athletes often reminds me of Yann Martel's novel *Life of Pi*. It was recommended to me by one of my best friends since childhood, David Sandler—Dr. Sandler, as he's known now—who often suggests books for me to read. This time he had simply texted, "Try *Life of Pi*, it's you."

He was right.

The novel tells the story of Pi, a lone shipwreck survivor stranded in a lifeboat with a dying zebra, a hyena, and a four-hundred-pound tiger named Richard Parker, all from his father's zoo. He would survive on the raft only if he could somehow train Richard Parker. He tamed him by first provoking him, then blowing his whistle while dropping anchor and rocking the boat until the tiger felt ill, teaching the tiger to associate the sound with seasickness. Pi established a place for himself on the boat the same way, giving Richard Parker room but enforcing his dominion over his own space. Ultimately Pi grew close to the tiger and even shared with it the food he took from the sea.

I learned to coexist with Bron, CP, Melo, KD, Dwight, and the other Richard Parkers of the NBA by carving out my territory on the raft. I recognize the power they hold as CEOs of their empires, the camaraderie they seek from other tigers in other dens, their daily need to prove their greatness and mark their domain, and the ferociousness it takes to become the best. I acknowledge their ability to sense fear and feed on opportunity, whether that means exposing the rookie who guards them, commanding the ball on a mismatch, dismissing the voice of an inexperienced coach, demanding the last shot despite a terrible shooting percentage that evening, disrupting the offense when they see an opening, chasing a dream at any cost, ignoring the less talented and productive, and exploiting situations for their benefit. Vying for the tiger's affection would have secured my immediate death, but showing my importance in its life and building trust along the way could ensure my professional survival, at least for a short while.

LeBron James is the best player in the world, and so he will never tell you he doesn't dribble well or score as comfortably with his left hand. But it was my responsibility to see where he could improve and convey it to him in a manner that would get him to listen and, more important, get him to try. If you can't convey that message in whatever tone and language you speak, you don't stand a chance on the boat with Richard Parker. I imagine LeBron heard some of what I had to say, which meant I was slowly chipping away at the ego and pride that understand-ably protect a legend. All the trappings of stardom can inhibit the learning process and prevent stars from being vulnerable and transparent. That's why you have to create a space that's yours and not theirs—a sanctuary where you can dictate the parame-ters while being attuned to their feelings and learning patterns.

With only sixty seconds to send a message and ninety min-utes to leave a mark, I had to grab LeBron's attention, earn his respect, challenge him in ways that magnified his imperfections, and empower him to want more for himself and see me as inte-gral to his development. I had to do what others don't: provoke him, violate his personal space, dispose of any celebrity entitle-ment, ignore him when necessary, talk with him candidly, and hope he would start to wonder whether he'd been given the moniker of King James before it was earned. I hoped the same nose that can sniff fear would also let him sense how much I truly cared and wanted to see him maximize his amazing gifts.

I don't know exactly how I learned this way of communicat-ing with the game's best players. It's mostly a matter of instinct and faith.

I believe in faith more than in dreams. To me, faith involves feeling confident in what I hope for even when I can't see it. Dreams require a vivid destination. Dreams are when you aim for the stars; faith is the certainty that you'll reach one, even if it's not the one you originally had in mind.

I fell deeply, passionately in love with basketball when I was a child. The game spoke to me in ways I couldn't explain, and still can't. It consumed whatever time I could give it and more. I wanted to be a part of it on the highest level I could imagine.

I'm six feet tall and weigh about 175 pounds. I wear a five-o'clock shadow to offset the lack of hair on my head, which I shave bald. I look rather unassuming, especially when standing next to the NBA players I train; folks assume I'm either a super-fan or the athlete's accountant, lawyer, agent, financial advisor, or private security. Unless I'm in a training session, I'm relatively soft-spoken. I'm certainly not the guy jumping on Oprah's couch, wearing a lampshade on his head at the party, or double-fisting beers.

I'm understated, respectful, and polite, usually a person who stands on the periphery during social gatherings. I'm reserved, not shy; I prefer to listen than to talk. I observe, I don't ignore; I assess, I don't judge.

I live a blessed life, a life of wonder and amazement. I understand why people who meet me want to ask the inevitable questions: *How did you create this life for yourself? Why do the best players in the world listen to you? What's your secret?*

I don't know what to tell them. They don't know about my journey, starting with a religious upbringing that placed no value on athletic accomplishment, winding through some false starts and missteps along roads I did not love, and ending up where I belong—helping the best athletes on the planet become even better at their chosen game.

I am fortunate. I have a gift, an ability to connect with and understand the people I work with no matter how different their backgrounds might be from mine. I don't train and teach by a system, and you won't find any paint-by-numbers instructions here that will enable you to do the things I do.

Except . . .

I work from my heart.

I pay attention.

I trust my instincts.

I have the privilege of seeing some of the true athletic wonders of the world in close quarters, seeing how hard they work to condition their bodies and refine their skills. Make no mistake, these players are all Ferraris, their engines responsive and explosive, all highly tuned and supple and sometimes temperamental.

I wonder too, every now and then, how exactly I got to be with them.

I can't tell you how to follow my path.

But I can describe the path I followed, in the hope you'll be inspired to find and follow your own.

CHAPTER TWO

RITUALS

ritual can b kryptonite 2 your dreams
#bcareful

I grew up in a Conservative Jewish home, child of an Israeli-born mother and Russian-born father who met and married in New York City. They were raised in observant families and chose Jewish education as their careers. Both taught some form of Judaic Studies to middle school and high school students at Jewish schools and synagogues. They spoke mostly Hebrew to me; my older sister, Mairav; and my younger sister, Aynat. We generally answered in English unless we didn't want someone to overhear our conversation. Our lives, like their incomes, were modest.

We were fairly observant, but not as observant as my father's family, who mostly lived in Hasidic-only neighborhoods and followed Judaic laws intensely and unquestioningly. We kept kosher at home, only eating food in accordance with Jewish law:

meat from cloven-hooved animals that chew their cud; non-predatory birds that had an extra toe, a crop, and a gizzard; fish with fins and scales. The animals we did eat, mammals and fowl, had to be slaughtered by a trained person using a nonserrated sharp knife and a single continuous cutting movement that severed the jugular vein, carotid artery, esophagus, and trachea to avoid causing the animal unnecessary pain. We purchased our groceries at kosher supermarkets.

I attended a small Jewish middle school and high school on the outskirts of Washington, DC, so rituals were part of my daily life. The boys wore yarmulkes, even on field trips to the Kennedy Center and the Smithsonian. We wore long pants and shirts with sleeves that fell to our elbows. We devoted thirty minutes each morning to prayer. When we turned thirteen, we had our bar mitzvahs, and from then on we would strap *tefillin* (small boxes containing Biblical verses) around our foreheads and arms and would wear *tallitot* (prayer shawls) each morning while reciting the prayers.

We took a dual load of mainstream core classes and Judaic Studies classes, covering Hebrew, Old Testament, Rabbinical Studies, and Jewish History. At the time, the school had no cafeteria, so we brought kosher lunches from home. We sang the Israeli national anthem at assembly. We were dismissed early on Fridays during the winter months to coincide with the early start of the Sabbath at sundown. There were no sporting events or school dances on Friday evenings or Saturdays until sundown. Ritual touched every part of my day, from what was in the refrigerator to the structure of my week.

Still, there were sports at school, and basketball was the one that took hold of me. I started to get serious about it in seventh grade, when the junior high coach didn't include my name on the roster he posted on his office door after tryouts. I was sure it had been a mistake; I was angry and frustrated, and I began to teach myself the game in earnest.

In the beginning I wasn't very good. Like most kids, I didn't know how to shoot properly or dribble with my left hand, but I just kept practicing on my own whenever I could. Free time was hard to find: I was in school from 8:15 A.M. to 4:30 P.M. while taking six honors and advanced placement classes and four Judaic Studies classes, generally taught in Hebrew. Still, I gave to the game whatever free time I had.

I shot baskets alone at the park, chased down my missed shots, dribbled in the garage, and ran sprints afterward even on the coldest nights. I wanted to improve, but I didn't know anyone who could help me. I didn't have access to any traditional basketball resources—no coaches, mentors, or trainers. I came up with my own drills, which I followed every single day regardless of the hour or the weather.

I grabbed inspiration wherever I could. I spent the summer tweaking my jump shot so it mirrored the ones I saw in photos in *Sports Illustrated*. I practiced my ball-handling based on what I had once seen Isiah Thomas of the Detroit Pistons do to warm up before a game. I ran sprints so I could run "like the wind," a phrase I heard a television announcer use to describe the Los Angeles Lakers' Byron Scott. I ran hills at the park after hearing that Walter Payton of the Chicago Bears and Jerry Rice of the San Francisco 49ers included this in their off-season workouts. I skipped rope because the boxers I watched on *ABC's Wide World of Sports* did so to improve their footwork.

The playground became like a movie theater where I took a basketball as my date. I wondered sometimes if I had some form of attention deficit disorder because I could never fully concentrate in the classroom or when reading and preparing my homework—yet an earthquake couldn't distract me when it came to basketball.

The small, private school I attended was twenty-five minutes away from our home, and my family didn't have much in common with the other families in our neighborhood. We were an immigrant family who didn't celebrate Halloween or Christmas, host sleepovers, visit the mall on the weekends, wear stylish clothes, attend sleepaway camp, watch football on Sundays, spend summers at the shore, dine out, belong to the community pool, or pretty much do anything else that mainstream American families do. Making friends in the neighborhood wasn't easy. I was never the popular kid and it didn't matter to me. I was perfectly happy practicing alone in the park a few blocks from my house. Basketball didn't force my parents to spend money they didn't have; the game was free and required only a ball and a rim. The simplest things excited me: hearing the bounce of a ball; seeing a new long white net hanging from a rim; practicing my jump shot on the goal draped over the garage of our home; running my fingers over the seams of a wet basketball after I shot in the rain; mimicking any new move I had seen on television.

I played varsity for most of my high school career. Perhaps because I was single-minded, self-taught, and sensitive about the game I loved, I had trouble with the head coach. I wasn't very good at first, and he ridiculed me in front of my teammates. He said I was slow and insisted I run all alone at the end of practice when I couldn't finish the team sprints within the allotted time. He called other players by their first name, but I was always "Ravin."

He required us to wear dress shoes to school on game days. I explained that money was tight and the purchase would force my parents to overextend.

"Come on, Ravin, shoes aren't that expensive," he replied.

My mother wouldn't budge, nor would he, so I found a pair of old black wing tips in my father's closet. I wore the shoes as little as possible, removing them immediately and slipping on the sneakers I carried in my backpack when I knew I wouldn't see the coach in the hallways during the school day.

Throughout my junior year he jerked around my playing

minutes, even benching me for an entire game with no explanation. I sat on the bench holding back tears, trying to understand why. I was so worked up that the next game I took every shot I could and scored forty-two points—the most ever at the school and enough to win me "County Player of the Week" honors. After that, I played with complete disregard for his words and his system.

I hated the guy—strong words, I know, but I loved the game and he was fucking with the only thing that mattered to me. I developed a huge chip on my shoulder. I vowed to become the best player he had ever seen. I would force him to eat his words.

I ramped up my training. I never missed a day or an opportunity to improve some aspect of my game. I would improvise even when I didn't have access to a basket or a court. I bounded up any staircase I could find, driving my knees as high as I could on each jump to improve my explosiveness. I dribbled between parked cars to practice keeping the ball close to my body. I ordered by mail a pamphlet that discussed plyometric training and promised to improve my quickness and vertical leap. I spent thirty minutes each night in the basement working on the drills: squat jumps, lunge jumps, line jumps, wall squats, and toe raises.

I'd lie in bed practicing the follow-through on my jump shot. The ball would leave my hand, forced upward by the flexion of my right wrist, gently kiss the ceiling, and then descend into my waiting fingers without my having to move my outstretched arm. I shoveled the snow to make a small walkway where I could practice handling the ball despite the frigid temperature. The cold, in fact, was the point: I wanted my hands to feel numb so I would struggle to control the ball. I ran countless sprints at the park near my house in the cold and in the dead of night after basketball practice because I wanted to immunize myself to the notion of fatigue.

There weren't enough notebooks at the local Rite Aid to log all the hours I spent practicing. Eventually I became the best player on my high school team and in the conference. My head didn't get big, though; I knew our league was at the bottom of the basketball food chain. I wasn't proud of my successes. I didn't wear a high school letterman's jacket. I didn't tell people where I played.

Basketball meant everything to me, but it was never a priority for my family, my teammates, or the school administration. To my parents, basketball was a hobby; for my teammates, it was a résumé builder; for the school, it was an extracurricular program.

Our team practiced only twice a week, because we had limited gym time and space. We didn't practice on the weekends and couldn't schedule Friday night games against better teams because of the Sabbath. We didn't hold open gyms. We didn't have fall or summer practice. Players couldn't use the gym in the early morning hours before school. We didn't have a weight room or warm-ups or pregame shootaround. We didn't watch game film. I could go on and on, but the simple fact was I lived in a world of ritual that had little use for anything outside its traditional concerns.

I attended Jewish schools, had Jewish friends, and played ball at the Jewish Community Center. Basketball was my passion and my only glimpse of the secular world. But sports of any kind were foreign to my parents and to their community, which was built around the customs of old. I began to resent religion. I couldn't imagine living a life where your passions are restrained by an ancient set of rules.

A few small-college basketball programs inquired about me, sending brochures and information requests to my coach. My mom didn't permit me to respond. Choosing a college because I could play ball there made no sense to immigrant parents whose sole focus was academics, as you can imagine.

"Are you crazy?" she said in her thick Israeli accent. "What are you going to be? A basketball player when you grow up?"

Ritual won. I listened to my parents and buried organized basketball in my backyard after high school.

I still remember how I felt after my last game. It was a Sunday afternoon in early spring. We had just defeated a Jewish school from New Jersey. I sat in the locker room as my teammates showered and changed. They were in a hurry to leave. I reluctantly removed my jersey and shorts. I methodically folded my uniform and placed it with my sneakers in a plastic bag. I didn't shower. In fact, I never showered after games; my conditioning was so fantastic I could play for hours without breaking a sweat, taking a sip of water, or feeling winded.

Before I left the locker room that day, I closed my eyes to snap a picture in my head so I would never forget the yellow lockers, the scent of Ben-Gay, the tiled floors, the two wood benches on which the team would gather to hear the game plan, the humming sound coming from the faulty lights, and the small off-white sweatband I wore on my right wrist. My teammates were relieved the season was over. This was a hobby to them; they had already moved on and were talking about family vacations and exams. I said nothing. I couldn't believe the most important thing I had known for the last several years was over.

CHAPTER THREE

PROVERBS 10:4

if it came easy we wouldn't want it
#noguarantees

My parents insisted we stay close to home for college. Private schools and out-of-state tuition were too expensive for us. I went to the University of Maryland, in College Park, about twenty-five miles from where I grew up.

Despite the academic demands—or maybe because of them—I still skipped rope, ran sprints, and practiced every day on my own. Organized basketball might have been behind me, but the game was still alive in intramurals, parks, playgrounds, and rec centers.

The fall of my freshman year I overheard a few students at the cafeteria discussing walk-on tryouts for the men's basketball team. There were more than forty thousand students at the university, so I could only imagine how many would participate.

On October 15 at midnight, more than one hundred aspiring

college basketball players packed Cole Field House for walk-on tryouts. I recognized some of the faces from pickup games on campus. For the first time I stood on a Division I arena floor. I had only played in small, dimly lit, beat-up, and empty gyms and auditoriums. It was magical simply to stand on the court, to feel the wood under my feet, to play in an arena that could house thousands of fans, to shoot on a beautifully manicured basket, to dribble a ball with the perfect amount of air, and to jump from a floor that offered just the right amount of give, adding a couple of inches to my vertical leap.

The assistant coaches divided us into groups and directed us to different stations on the court to evaluate our ball-handling and shooting. From there, they split us into smaller groups so they could watch us play full-court five on five. I wasn't surprised I played well. I was only a couple of months removed from three years of varsity ball. Every few minutes the coaches would cut a few players and tell them to take a seat in the stands. After nearly an hour, the assistant coaches had whittled the group down to ten players. They divided us into two teams of five and we played full-court on the main floor. After the game, we remained on the floor, waiting to hear our fate.

An assistant coach whose name escapes me tapped me on the shoulder. He asked me my name, and then where I'd gone to high school.

"Charles E. Smith Jewish Day School," I told him.

"You played where?" he said, chuckling.

I repeated myself.

"Never heard of it. Where's that at? You said Jewish, right?"

I nodded.

"Wish I knew about you before these tryouts."

It turned out that five of the players standing with me at half-court had already spoken to the coaching staff about walk-on positions and had been promised roster spots. Coming from my cocoon, I'd had no idea such a thing was possible, no idea that people could game the system that way so that the whole tryout felt something like a sham.

"I wish I would have known about you earlier," he said. "I like your game. I'm impressed."

He paused. "Would you want to be a manager this year?" he asked.

I replied immediately: "No."

I was a basketball player, not a water boy, equipment manager, or statistician, and I wasn't going to hold clipboards or pass out towels just so I could spend time with a program and around athletes I felt like I could compete against.

So there it was: I was the last player cut from walk-on tryouts at a major Division I university. I grabbed the gym bag I had tossed near the bleachers when I arrived. I left Cole Field House and began to walk back to my dorm. I was devastated. I had come so close, only to lose out because I didn't know and couldn't have known how the game was really played.

The words *Goddamn Jewish school* echoed through my brain.

Thinking about that moment reminds me of the movie *Sliding Doors* with Gwyneth Paltrow. The plot splits into two parallel universes, based on the two paths her life could take, depending on whether she catches a London Underground train or not. If only I would have been the fifth guy to make that roster rather than being the last guy cut, my dream would have come true. My life would have instantly changed.

I cried that night. I was crushed. Hard work was supposed to create wealth and dreams, said Proverbs 10:4, but it hadn't for me. I was good enough, and that assistant coach said so; who knows how much better I might have become with the resources of a Division I program—trainers, weight rooms, film study, coaching, and teaching—available to me for the first time? But unless I was from a prestigious high school basketball powerhouse or had a letter of reference from an influential coach, the institution of basketball wasn't willing to give me a chance.

Having those things on a résumé mattered more than what I could do.

I loved the game too much to stop playing, so I continued to play and practice on my own. I went from playground to playground in some of the roughest neighborhoods in the Washington, DC, metropolitan area, hunting for the best competition.

I was naïve at first. After a childhood filled with religion, I assumed everyone had good intentions and basketball would keep me out of harm's way. It didn't. After several hard fouls, taunts from the tough guys, and a strong punch that nearly fractured my orbital bone, I became more sensible and a better judge of situations and character. I grew more guarded and calculating with my conversation, body language, and actions. I curtailed the small talk at the playground and instead simply nodded my head or extended my hand for a quick fist-pound to the other players I recognized.

Less was more. I came across as confident and even aloof to some. The playground didn't respect softness and sensitivity. Bolder was better, so I didn't retreat on the court. At the same time, I didn't sacrifice my identity or authenticity to try to blend into the environment. I didn't chase racial stereotypes to convince others I was "down." You know what I'm referring to: the white kid who speaks with his "blaccent," changing his speech patterns, interests, and dress when around the African-American community.

In time I became familiar with playground culture, its slang, and the free style of play that focused on isolations and creating off the dribble. I learned to ask, "Who got next?" when I arrived at the park, and then demand they include me as part of their five even though they'd already decided I couldn't play just because of how I looked. *Ain't no way this preppy-ass white boy wit' all that fuckin' hair can hoop* was written on their faces when I asked for next. (Back then I had a mountain of dirty-blond wavy hair cut short on the sides and long on top.)

Despite its diversity, sport has never been free of stereotypes and assumptions. Fans, media, teams, and even players make judgments based on appearance all the time. It didn't surprise me the fellas at the park assumed either I couldn't play or, if I could, I would simply stand on the perimeter to shoot jump shots. They soon learned I didn't play that way. I was quick and fast. I played most of the game with the ball in my hands and I handled the ball extremely well. I created off the dribble, attacked the basket, played with flair and personality. I talked shit—creative shit.

"Cookies," I'd say as I backpedaled downcourt with a bit of a gallop after sinking a shot.

I played hard yet respectfully when competing against the tough street guys. I stood firm on my foul calls, demanded the ball, and found comfort in my own skin being a distinct minority on the playground and in the community. I bowled in my lane, played well, and left my fingerprints on courts throughout the city. The summer gave me the chance to measure myself against many of the top college players who were home for a few months. I became a really good player. But the question *What team do you play for?* always stung.

My sophomore year I went through another tryout for an entirely new coaching staff; head coach Bob Wade had been replaced by Ohio State's Gary Williams, who brought in a whole new set of assistants. Once again I made it to the last group, and I think part of the reason I got cut this time is that I'd been spending so much time on the playgrounds and my game had become more individualistic, flashier. It's not that I couldn't play a more buttoned-down style, but I think they looked at me and asked themselves if this was what they wanted from a potential walk-on guard.

And that was the end of my story as a player in organized ball.

I still logged thousands of minutes in parks and rec centers around the city. If they retired jerseys at the playground, then RAVIN would have hung from a light pole draped over the mid-court line. Four years passed by quicker than I could say, *Next point wins.*

I graduated with degrees in both Finance and Marketing. When deciding what to do after college, I thought law school seemed like the most natural progression. I had known rules and ritual for much of my life; law school represented the logical step in a life largely regulated by code and custom. I applied, was accepted, and started law school in San Diego the following fall.

At first I didn't mind the study and the long hours. But eventually I started picturing a life handcuffed to a desk, dispassionately working on cases that didn't interest me, billing clients in six-minute intervals to justify my salary. No way. I couldn't do it.

Whether it was Judaic custom, Judaic laws, or American jurisprudence, it was all the same to me. It was ritual and rules that serve to inhibit dreams and demonstrate our distrust of one another. *We need rules to keep us in order. We need rules to help us remember our past. We need rules to help us find a connection with God.* Maybe the underlying purpose was to create order and make freedom possible, but all they did for me was to make me feel like a prisoner. Imagine if I invited you to my home for a week when I went out of town, and I left you the keys on the kitchen counter along with a note that said, "Feel free to stay as long as you want, just please do not sit on the couch, use my remote, sleep in my bed, use my restroom, cook on my stove, bake with my oven, or drive my car."

As I had always done, I turned to the game when I felt lost and alone. After my first year of law school, I began to find time in between all my schoolwork and classes to practice and play again. While my classmates positioned themselves for law review, summer associate positions, clerkships, and ultimately, jobs with good firms, I snuck away from the library to play ball at a local rec center. Unlike my classmates, with their mature and responsible goals, I dreamt of living a life doing only what I loved. I knew I loved basketball. But I had no idea what I could do with it.

So, in the meantime, I did what I was supposed to do. I continued to study and to pray.

CHAPTER FOUR

BREAKING IN

don't confuse what u're supposed 2 do
with what u're intended 2 do
#destiny

I graduated from California Western School of Law in 1996 and practiced for nearly three years with a midsize firm in Southern California, chained to the law library and my office. It was everything I thought it would be: long hours, crappy pay, stifling environments, passive-aggressive supervisors, difficult colleagues, uninspiring personalities, and fantastically boring work.

The office was filled with lawyers with four- and five-letter first names who claimed Irish descent and had served in the American military. Some of the partners suggested we give ourselves Irish names for the St. Patrick's Day office celebration. They took pride in their starched white shirts, red ties, blue blazers, and shined cordovan wing tips. They honored their weekend military reserve commitments and went hunting on their vacations. They wrapped white napkins around their bottles of Guinness during happy hour and sang Irish tunes when hammered. They all decorated their offices with their diplomas, some family photos, and plants. I didn't fit in, and I didn't want to.

I came to work each morning feeling anxious, unmotivated, and lost. Having spent so much of my youth in religious studies, I turned to the familiar whenever I felt down. I would close my eyes at my desk each morning and beg God for answers. I wanted Him to send a lightning bolt through the ceiling with a yellow Post-it attached containing a blueprint for my future. No such bolts were forthcoming, at least not in the form I hoped for.

I spoke with my mom at length. She suggested I hated law because of the office and the type of law I practiced. I looked into the possibility of transitioning to some form of entertainment law. I thought it might be interesting because it would involve intellectual property, contracts, corporations, and tax—courses I could at least tolerate in school. I lived in Southern California, so I figured there could be many opportunities. I attended seminars and conferences in this practice area on the weekends. When I arrived I found hundreds of lawyers and law students dressed fashionably and all trying to shove their résumés down the throat of the lecturer. The attendees seemed mostly interested in the parties they hoped to attend, filled with clients they hoped to represent. I wasn't like these people either; I just wanted to do the work and feel productive in an environment I enjoyed.

While still at the firm, I began toying with the idea of becoming an NBA agent. At first blush it seemed like a natural fit considering my passion for the game, and I could understand the legal, insurance, and financial nuances associated with negotiating an NBA player contract.

Unbeknownst to my employer, in the evenings and weekends I started prospecting for clients in my old backyard. I knew a few players from my days on the playground, and I called Johnny Rhodes, who had played basketball at the University of Maryland. I volunteered to help him with anything he needed. He hoped to latch on with an NBA team and hadn't had much success to date. To my surprise he agreed. We didn't sign any paperwork, and I assumed there were other people in his circle still trying to help him—still, in my eyes I had my first client, even though I had no idea where to begin.

I studied NBA rosters whenever I could take a break, to see where Johnny might have the best chance of making a team. I drafted letters and contacted those teams' general managers and directors of player personnel in an effort to introduce Johnny to them.

I figured that physical talent was not a scarce commodity in the NBA, so I highlighted Johnny's unselfishness and the team chemistry it would help create. After a few weeks of letters and phone calls, I persuaded the Washington Bullets to invite him to veterans' camp. I called Johnny to share the news; he thanked me a hundred times over the phone. This was his dream. And I finally felt some satisfaction and happiness with my work.

I paid $1,500, an enormous expense for me at the time, to register with the National Basketball Players Association as a certified player agent, a necessary credential if I were going to negotiate Johnny's NBA contract. After only a couple of weeks, Washington released Johnny. He didn't call me to tell me; the team did. I phoned him several times over the next week. No response. I finally reached his mother, who explained he had signed with a team in China. I was startled. I had just spent so much time and money I didn't have in an effort to help him, and he hadn't extended me the courtesy of a phone call.

Still, Johnny's dash to China didn't discourage me. Nothing in life had come easy to me, so I figured I was destined to trip and fall a few more times before I found my footing. I continued to allocate a few hours each week to the hunt for clients.

One Friday in late spring I called in sick so I could travel to Arizona to attend an NBA pre-draft camp, hoping there would be a potential client or maybe some nonlaw basketball opportunities for me. Agents, runners, financial advisors, NBA personnel, unemployed coaches, and groupies filled the lobby of the Tucson hotel. I recognized players' faces from television, but I didn't personally know anyone there. As players came in and out of the hotel lobby, some agent, manager, handler, or runner would immediately glom onto them like mice scrounging for scraps. It seemed like many of the players already knew these people.

I realized these guys had probably been in these players' ears for a while, spending money on them to win their affection. If that was the price of admission, I was sunk. I couldn't even afford a rental car in Tucson or a room at the same hotel as the players and teams. I would have to improvise and distinguish myself if I wanted to land a client. Instead of smoke and mirrors, I decided to just be me, nothing more and nothing less.

I've never been timid or lacking in confidence, so I targeted the biggest and baddest players at the camp, literally and figuratively. On the second day, I approached 6-9, 290-pound Jahidi White at the arena on the Arizona campus. Jahidi had recently finished his senior season at Georgetown, and I figured I would at least find some DC connection with him. I can't recall what I first said, but the conversation eventually shifted to the parks and summer leagues we both knew back east. I invited him to lunch the next day. He agreed.

The following day I was waiting for Jahidi in the lobby of the hotel when I heard someone call my name. I looked around and saw a guy I'll call Ron, a familiar face from playing ball on the DC playgrounds. Ron said hello and filled me in on his business and the clients he represented. He managed a few professional basketball players we both knew who were currently playing overseas. He gave me his firm's brochure, and we exchanged contact information.

After my lunch with Jahidi—he ate like a horse, and the bill made me swallow hard—I met up with Ron to discuss whether there were any consulting opportunities with his company. I thought I could help procure marketing deals for his athletes, create recruiting brochures, or evaluate potential clients. He said he'd think about it, but we should keep in touch. I was disappointed, mostly because I was so desperate to find something to break the funk I was in. Sunday evening I flew home to Southern California without a new client: Jahidi had signed with David Falk, best known as the agent for Michael Jordan and Patrick Ewing.

Monday morning I was back in the office. I sat at my desk and stared at the computer screen. I closed my eyes hoping to hear the lightning bolts crash into my desk, not caring if they hit me too.

CHAPTER FIVE

BREAKING OUT

it feels good b/c the heavens have shared w/u your destiny
#listen

I t had become my habit to try to self-medicate before heading into work by stopping at the local YMCA for some early morning exercise. One day I was finishing up my routine—run, swim, shower, shave, properly loop tie, fold handkerchief, button cuff links, lace the wing tips—when I spotted a flyer someone had posted on the board near the gym doors.

HEAD COACHES WANTED, it said.

I didn't have a cell phone, so I jotted down the number and called it the minute I arrived at the office. I spoke with someone and learned that there was a boys' basketball league looking for help. I volunteered immediately.

I wasn't sure if the law firm's managing partner would approve of my leaving the office early one night a week to coach a thirteen-and-under basketball team, so I decided to couch my

efforts as community service and business development. I asked
if he would be willing to pay a couple hundred dollars for the
team jerseys and, in exchange, I'd include the name of his firm
and its phone number on the back of the jerseys. To my surprise,
he agreed.

I had to laugh when I saw the thirteen-year-old boys wearing their green jerseys with an ad for a law firm stenciled on
their backs. It reminded me of the lawyers who run television
commercials pursuing clients to add to their asbestos and meso-
thelioma class-action suits.

I had never trained or coached anyone, so I didn't have any
scripted plans for practice. I figured I would improvise based on
the energy level of the kids and whether I thought the drills had
to be tapered down depending on their ability. I wanted them to
run on every drill. In my experience conditioning mattered, especially with unskilled players. After all, if an unskilled player
can run all day, then he can at least defend and frustrate his opponent. I hoped these kids would become quicker, faster, and
better conditioned than the other kids in the YMCA league, so I
incorporated some form of running into every basic layup, shooting, and passing drill. I was asking a lot from young boys, but if
they loved the game, they would see it as a chance to improve.

At the end of practice, I added a few stationary ball-handling
drills I had designed when I played. These drills were an early
version of the one I introduced LeBron James to in New Orleans. They forced the kids to alter the velocity and rhythm of
their dribbles as they stood in place, head up, knees bent, chest
up; they had to dribble the ball high and fast, high and slow, low
and fast, and low and slow. Think of the sound the ball makes
when it bounces on the wood floor, like a stick striking a drum.
The ball creates a beat. If the beats from the dribble are too sym-
metrical and repetitive, a good defender will time the beats to
anticipate a steal. But if the offensive player can alter the rhythm,
the defensive player has to guess the next beat. I had played pi-

ano for several years, so it made sense to me to compare dribbling to music; also, the kids loved music, and most of it
emphasized the beat. They always listened and did their best to
mimic the drills. They did whatever I asked. I don't recall if they
even asked for water breaks.

We played every Saturday. We won every game.

After a few weeks of practice, parents would tell me they had
never seen their kids so engaged and excited. They described
their kids as "spazzy," "hyper," and "difficult." They wondered
what I was doing that they could replicate. I honestly didn't
know. I figured I just knew more about the game than some volunteer father coaching his son's team.

At the end of the season, a parent asked if I could come an
hour before practice to meet the team outside the rec center.
When I arrived, I learned from another parent that the players
had pooled their allowance money to throw me a surprise pizza
party. "Surprise" was an understatement. Thirteen-year-old boys
buy video games with their allowance money; they don't throw
parties for adults they barely know.

A few weeks later a paralegal in my office told me her son
had written an essay about the person he admired the most.

"Who is that?" I said.

"You," she replied.

"Are you serious?" I said.

I'd spent only a couple of hours each week with these kids.
We didn't talk about their personal lives, family lives, or even
school lives. We focused strictly on basketball during those limited hours. I don't know what I did or said that resonated with
these kids. I figured I must have inherited the teaching gene
from my educator parents.

Or maybe it was that I loved what I was doing, and was excited to share some of my knowledge. At that moment, I could
tear off my disguise, use every layer of my personality on a task
for the first time, and even bring my passion to my work. It was

a great feeling, and the contrast made life back at the law firm that much harder to endure.

One morning I submitted a brief to one of the partners. He called me to his office and began asking me the same question over and over, each time raising his voice another decibel. I had grown tired of his and the other partner's shit over the years. They were condescending and offensive. When I first interviewed for the job, the managing partner asked me, "Are you one of those Jews who would take the day off for Yom Kippur?" After asking my parents' nationality, he said, "There will always be war between Palestinians and Israelis, but the World Series is what matters right now."

Over the years at this firm I bit my lip and debated whether to call the California Bar to complain. I never shot back with what I really wanted to say, no matter how outrageous, inappropriate, and baseless their comments were. This was my first real job, and I figured I was supposed to eat crow.

But this time, I just lost it.

"Why are you busting my balls?" I snapped. "If you want me to change it, I will. If you don't want me to change it, then I won't. Just tell me what you want!"

He picked up his phone and dialed the office manager's extension. I knew what that meant. I stormed out of his office. In less than twenty minutes I packed up my belongings, dumping binders of memos and pleadings I had drafted into the trash, and resigned. I sat through an exit interview where I was given the option of resignation or termination. I chuckled inside when the partners compared my time at the firm with how Barry Bonds didn't fit in with certain teams.

I felt so relieved it was over. I hated the office, the lawyers, and the work. It was like ten thousand pounds of dog shit had been miraculously removed from the bottoms of my favorite Air Jordan 3s.

CHAPTER SIX

FREE AGENT

a 6th sense we should trust more often
#intuition

I moved back east and back home. My parents lived about thirty minutes outside of Washington, DC. I called Ron to inform him I had a few hours a week to help him with his business. For some reason, he now agreed. He and his business partner had signed consensus All-American Steve Francis from the University of Maryland, a big coup considering they didn't represent many top-tier athletes; Steve was sure to be a top pick in the upcoming NBA draft.

They felt Steve needed some help with the mechanics of his shot, so they retained an NBA assistant coach to work with him. In a suit and tie, I sat for two days in the gym of a local high school to watch Steve work on his jumper. The coach insisted Steve hold his follow-through on the release and not dip the ball below his chest after catching a pass. He gave him a few drills to work on these fundamentals. I agreed with the diagnosis but thought most everything else was nonsense. The sessions seemed too long, resembled a monologue, lacked intensity, and included too little collaboration with the student/player. I left the gym unimpressed after my first glimpse of NBA coaching and training.

Like me, Steve was easily distracted. I watched him play with his cell phone and swivel his head whenever he heard the gym doors open. He had a short attention span, so I couldn't imagine he would get much out of the coach's lecture. I found out that he loved movies, so I figured he was more visual and could learn better from demonstration and participation.

The coach insisted Steve take fifteen hundred shots a day. Anyone will become a better shooter if they take fifteen hundred shots a day; it's simply a matter of creating neural patterns, whether they're correct or incorrect, through repetition. I'll bet you a turkey sandwich on whole wheat with lettuce and tomato that if you take fifteen hundred underhanded shots each day over the course of a summer, even you will soon become a solid underhanded stationary shooter.

But what are you practicing for? A shooting contest, with racks of balls and no defenders? Or a game of movement and flow played at high speed?

The NBA didn't need better stationary shooters. It needed players who could knock down shots taken at game speed. It struck me that a better way to develop that skill would be to practice it in short, well-defined training sessions using more complex drills to mimic or even exaggerate game conditions. Incorporating more movement into the repetitions would simultaneously challenge the brain, senses, heart, and lungs, while also creating new neural pathways. Don't ask me how I knew this. It was just something that occurred to me as I watched Steve Francis go through this one-dimensional training.

I understood the value of repetition with proper form. But a player was far more likely to master these movements and perform them intuitively in the high-stress atmosphere of an NBA game if he practiced them with high intensity and with a high level of sensory overload. This isn't golf, where the whole world gets quiet so a player can swing; it's a game played at a frenetic pace, in front of screaming fans, a high-strung head coach, overbearing veterans who demand the ball, and camera crews capturing every second. The drills should also add elements of conditioning, to force the player to move properly and efficiently even when his nervous system wants to revert to old habits because of fatigue. I didn't understand why this coach put skills into one box and conditioning in another, when the game requires the constant application of both at once. Combining all these variables into a player's training would help him develop the abilities he really needed.

I didn't share any of these thoughts with the NBA assistant or with Steve's manager. I simply filed them away in my subconscious for future use.

It only took a few weeks for me to grow restless with the consulting project. The agency side of things didn't feel right to me. There were a lot of shady characters on the street who feigned influence on players. There was too much babysitting involved, and a general lack of professionalism and honesty from so many in the industry I had met. Advisors, players, families, and friends would ask for favors with no intention of reciprocating or honoring a quid pro quo. The agent/management game was often capital-intensive and high-risk; paid its staff with things like event tickets rather than reasonable salaries; and everything depended on the whims of clients, who often ignored advice and made knee-jerk decisions.

So becoming an agent wasn't for me, even if it was the most obvious way to combine my legal background with my basketball passion. I gave it a brief try. I had my fill. It wasn't the answer I hoped for, so I went back to my search.

CHAPTER SEVEN

NO COINCIDENCES

they turn 2 u 4 what u know, not 4 what u don't
#wisdom

I had absolutely no idea what to do with my life. I continued to live at home to save money and to give me some flexibility with the job search. I read every self-help book at Barnes & Noble and left stacks of them piled on tables at the store. I made lists of possible jobs in sports, finance, and marketing that I thought I could tolerate. I debated going back to school, but I couldn't imagine incurring additional student loans.

My mom put me in touch with a few people she knew, hoping they could point me in the right direction. I took a meeting with a big-firm lawyer she thought might offer a different perspective on working in the law. I waited for him at a sandwich shop near his office.

"We're not hiring laterals," he mentioned as we stood in line.

"That will be nine sixty-nine, sir, for both sandwiches," the woman behind the register said.

I waited a few seconds. His hands remained in his pockets. I waited another second.

"Will that be cash or charge, sir?" she asked.

"Cash," I said as I left a ten-dollar bill on the counter and carried my tray to a window seat, my "advisor" trailing behind me.

I was getting nowhere. I was eager and running really fast, but in place and in heavy sand. My folks were losing patience. They're practical people and they all but begged me to return to law. After all, it was what I had studied and it was where I had most of my work experience. I lived under their roof and felt at least somewhat obliged to heed their advice.

If I couldn't find a job I loved, I could at least spend a couple of hours during the week surrounded by the thing I loved. I knew a few players from my playground days who'd recently graduated college and were preparing to play overseas. Perhaps inspired by watching Steve work with that NBA assistant coach, I suggested they meet me for a training session at the gym.

I had absolutely no agenda when I offered to help Darren and Jason. All I wanted was to spend time in the gym to help mute my unhappiness. The possibility that training basketball players could ever become a business was light-years away from my thoughts. Unbeknownst to me, my prayers were slowly being answered.

It was my first time in the gym training anyone other than some thirteen-year-old boys from suburbia. I approached it the same way I had with those boys: no script, improvising based on their energy and interest level. I don't know why or how, but I could always sense other people's emotions and gauge the intensity of their feelings, ever since I was a child.

Darren and Jason met me at a local high school. I had them skip rope to warm up and to fatigue them before we started the drill portion of the workout. Anyone can play fresh. Every player can make shots during warm-ups. I wanted to help them excel even when fatigued.

From there, I situated them along different parts of the court and led them through a few defensive drills that emphasized conditioning and reaction time. I relied strictly on my intuition and created drills that had a game context to keep them from losing interest and focus.

They were both small guards who had the ball in their hands most of the time; I made them run every sprint while dribbling a basketball. They performed agility and quickness drills with balls, in a defensive stance and in gamelike defensive situations. For instance, one stood near the lane and sprinted to challenge the shooter on the wing, then repeated this at the top of the key and again on the opposite wing. This was designed to improve their reaction time and their ability to close out on a shooter before the shot.

I assigned them ball-handling drills I had perfected in my parents' garage and at the park: mastering a series of moves (crossovers, between the legs, between the legs crossover, behind the back) during gamelike scenarios: on a fast break and half-court isolation. I quickly noticed their deficiencies because I recognized them in myself. I watched their eyes and torsos as they dribbled. They leaned their torsos too far forward, making them more likely to lose the ball and their balance. Also, this meant their backs were flexed, so it would take them longer to straighten up and shoot the ball if the defense left them open. If they looked at the ball when they dribbled, I knew they weren't completely comfortable handling it—and, more important, they couldn't see the court, their teammates, or the defenders.

They must have found the workouts challenging and helpful, because they asked if we could get together again. I had as much fun as they did. I couldn't wait to come back the following evening.

After those first sessions with Jason and Darren, I started

holding workouts at local rec centers and high school gyms more frequently because I had free time on my hands. Soon other guys from the DC area who play pro ball abroad started showing up, as well as some future NBA stars. It was basketball for basketball's sake: hard work and meaningful, but fun like a pickup game. There's just one degree of separation between college, international, and NBA players who live in the same city, and word of mouth led them all to find me.

I loved working with the players. I should rephrase that: This wasn't work to me. It was the furthest thing from work that I could imagine.

Steve Francis started attending my workouts because Darren and Jason were friends of his. He got into the spirit of them right away; as part of each session, he would cup his hands to clap and yell, "Let's get activated!" in his deep baritone voice, which always made him and his friends laugh. He encouraged Darren and Jason to push through even when they thought they had no more gas in the tank. He cheered for his friends as much as they cheered for him. He wasn't self-absorbed, and hoped his childhood friends would achieve the same kind of success as he would.

"Come on, Jo! Come on, Young'un. You got more in ya!" he'd yell from the sideline as he waited for his turn.

Steve was an incredible talent; he played just one year at Maryland after transferring from junior college, and was a finalist for the Wooden and Naismith awards as College Player of the Year. He wound up as the number-two pick in the 1999 NBA draft, won the NBA Rookie of the Year Award, and eventually played in three All-Star Games.

He spoke a hybrid of DC slang and Maryland suburban formality. The formality came from attending racially and demographically diverse county schools; the slang represented community, timeliness, and cultural relevance, and I knew it was a language I ought to learn if I wanted to get to know him. During our workouts he led by example, and his intensity practically bled onto the court. When a sprint drill required him to touch a line, he slapped it with the palms of both hands rather than giving it a slight drag of his fingers as the others would do initially.

After a couple of weeks he called me directly to schedule individual sessions. I was still very new to the NBA world, but I had questions about the traditional methods of draft preparation, which meant having him master a few drills he would perform for a team. It seemed shortsighted to me, like cramming for a quiz while ignoring the final exam that was a few days later. I thought he should focus on the parts of his game he could improve, with an eye on the summer league and his rookie season to come, rather than concentrate on those pre-draft drills.

Steve had the speed of an NFL wide receiver or defensive back, plus a forty-three-inch vertical leap. His remarkable athleticism allowed him to mask his imperfections on the court, since he could just run or jump past you, over you, or around you, and no one in college could match him. In the NBA he wouldn't have as much of a physical advantage. I wanted to raise his skill level to be on par with his athleticism, so I designed drills focusing on offensive efficiency, streamlining his jump shot, and improving his conditioning. Steve was the first NBA player I had worked with, so everything I did with him on the court was essentially trial and error. I taught myself on the fly and modified some of the drills I had designed for myself when I was younger.

Each drill was performed at game speed and involved covering the length of the court in a finite number of dribbles. If he could master the drill in ninety feet, he would certainly be able to do it in half the court. I assumed he would have the ball in his hands most of the game, so we used drills that involved beating a defender to the basket or shooting his jump shot from a distance of fifteen to twenty-four feet on the wings, at the top of the key, and in transition.

In games, Steve could usually attack the basket from any-where on the court and close with a dunk, but I wanted him to have other finishing options in case the dunk wasn't available—if he was in foul trouble and couldn't risk getting called for a charge; if a seven-foot center was in his way; if he was nursing a slight injury. We worked on releasing the ball in the lane with a high arc and limited ball rotation with either hand, like throwing a knuckleball in a basketball context. I suspected teams would assign long-armed and athletic players to defend him, so we fine-tuned his shot to make sure he didn't dip the ball below his chest after receiving a pass, which would allow his defender to swipe for the ball.

I considered Steve a "plus-one learner." That means he would master any drill after one practice round and immediately integrate the drill to game situations and perform it at game speed. I knew he would be a great NBA player. He was immensely talented, a world-class athlete, passionate about the game, and a tireless worker.

He wore his emotions on his sleeve. He had suffered a tragic loss as a teenager with the unexpected death of his mother. It took a toll on him for the next few years. He didn't play organized basketball in his junior or senior years as he bounced around a number of high schools, trying to regain his balance. Her death rattled him, and the aftershock left him more susceptible to outbursts and sensitivity. During our workouts he might yell with excitement when he did a drill particularly well, or kick a ball and curse when he faltered. In time, Steve became more candid, transparent, and trusting of me, which made him more receptive to learning and willing to try things on the court he had never done before. He even became more patient with me as from time to time he politely dismissed drills I proposed that he considered ineffective.

I encouraged him to make mistakes. The gym was our classroom: a place to experiment, learn, and grow without fear, since

I didn't control his playing time or paycheck. Mistakes led to improvement.

And I had the patience of Job with him, because it didn't seem right to berate him for being late or missing a workout or even to tell him not to be so hard on himself, when I recognized he subconsciously played the game he loved to restore some normalcy in his life. From my own experience, happiness on the court could soften the unhappiness off the court. I encouraged him to see the court as his personal sanctuary and to spend as much time there as he could, if only to find a peaceful place to address uncomfortable thoughts.

I never took an aggressive tone with him because I knew how poorly I responded to sarcasm and raised voices. I promised myself I would learn from my experiences, never become like the assholes I had worked for, and never allow the tone of my message to overwhelm the message itself. Our sessions were always collaborative, conversational, and filled with positive reinforcement.

I wanted Steve to add textures to his game, knowing he would inevitably play for different coaches with different philosophies and for teams with different rosters. The NBA coaching and player carousel rotates quickly. Losing coaches are fired midyear; even winning coaches can get fired at the end of the season; and every player, even an All-Star, can be traded. A new team or coach might demand from the player a dimension of his game that he wasn't used to showing.

Steve and I got along well. Like most players, he was macho and tough in public, but I sensed a tender and gentle side to him. We spent a lot of time talking about life and the blessings the game had given him. Steve loved his mother dearly and carried her driver's license in his wallet after she passed away. He was extremely generous with friends and family. He would surprise his younger sister with visits to her classroom in elementary school. He purchased a new home for his grandmother who raised him after his mother's death. He paid some bills for the parents of his childhood friends. He took his best friends with him wherever he went so they too could get the chance to walk in the clouds.

In late June of 1999, I attended the NBA draft at the MCI Center in Washington. I watched Steve shake hands with NBA commissioner David Stern as the Vancouver Grizzlies selected him with the second overall pick. Few could appreciate how hard he worked and how circuitous a route he took before landing in the NBA. I did, because his travels were unusual, like mine. We both pursued the unlikeliest of paths in search of happiness, and now our love for the game and our faith in a better life had caused our lives to come together, however briefly.

Throughout his rookie year I wrote him letters encouraging him to play with the freedom, recklessness, creativity, and love I'd witnessed the previous spring and summer. I feared his coaches would try to rein in his talent under the guise of their "system."

When Steve came back to DC for the summer after his rookie year in Houston, he called me to see if we could continue our workouts. I was happy to make time for him. I had no illusions that this was leading anywhere for me, and at the moment I didn't care. Happiness mattered, and I was happy that we were going to reconnect and get back onto the court to resume our training.

CHAPTER EIGHT

BREAKING THROUGH

u prayed 4 circles & the heavens sent rectangles;
trust me, they listened
#openmind #opportunityiseverywhere

With Steve Francis setting the league on fire as a rookie, I wondered if the time had come for me to try to edge my way into NBA circles. I thought that between my law degree, my early track record, and my innovative approach to training, surely some team would be interested in my services. My journey so far was an unusual one, but I assumed some general manager would recognize the value I could bring to an organization.

I followed what I believed to be the proper protocol and sent a résumé and cover letter to every team to introduce myself. I waited patiently for the call, the e-mail, the invitation to interview, and the job offer that was sure to come. It was only a matter of time, I thought. But one week became several months. I triple-checked the cover letters and résumés I had sent out to be certain they'd gone to the right people. I kept my phone by my side at all times, afraid I'd miss an important call. Eventually I received a few responses in the mail, which I quickly tore open, only to find standard rejection letters.

Everyone who ever touched a basketball wanted a job with an NBA team, and to an outsider looking in, it seemed that only members of the basketball establishment secured those positions. I was not part of their establishment. I didn't look like the establishment. I wasn't the son, grandson, brother, nephew, cousin, husband, former teammate, or childhood friend of the establishment. Electric-blue résumé paper and a sixteen-point font would not have stopped my submission from being consigned to the stack of random résumés received by NBA head coaches and general managers each week, not to mention the phone calls and glad-handing from every former player and coach, all hoping to return to the league.

Bowing to this reality, I had no real choice other than to give the law another chance. I did so reluctantly, still praying I could somehow make a life for myself doing what I loved. I wasn't going to repeat the mistake of my swan dive into a job from the ten-meter platform; instead I jumped, feet first, into the kiddie pool and applied for contract work, eventually finding a temporary assignment with a law firm.

The first day of the assignment I rode the subway to the office feeling anxious. A senior associate greeted me in the lobby and asked me to sign a nondisclosure agreement, and then handed me the pleadings he wanted me to review. We went in and found my temporary desk, at which I sat and began to read. A half hour later, I realized I was staring at the same line that I'd already read a hundred times. I went to the kitchen to prepare a cup of tea and tried to reassure myself things would be OK.

"Please, God. I can't do this forever," I prayed.

I procrastinated by wandering from the kitchen to the law

library. I browsed a law firm directory and learned that this contract assignment at Shearman & Sterling had placed me in one of the top firms in the world, made up of the best lawyers from the best schools with the best credentials. I wasn't a best lawyer from a best school with the best credentials. I certainly didn't belong here.

One day became one week became one month became many months. Apparently they approved of me and my work product, because they extended me an offer to join them full-time. I made the mature, responsible, and practical decision, accepting their offer.

My colleagues were great, the firm was great, they treated me great, and they paid me well. Compared to my California experience, it was as if I'd gone from the ghetto to the White House. But when we took off all the makeup, I was still practicing law, and law just didn't do it for me.

I used whatever free time I had to train any players who asked for my help. I loved seeing them smile with relief when they finally mastered a conditioning drill they'd feared, or toss a ball in the air in sheer joy when they incorporated a move we'd practiced into a competitive one-on-one drill, or control their breath following a grueling interval sprint around the perimeter of the court after we spoke about the importance of efficient breathing. I've always been interested in the science of performance; I liked to sit in a bookstore and read whatever I could find about exercise physiology, corrective exercise, and methods of training, looking to understand why something works and maybe how to make it work better. In a sense I was my own first experiment, and now I had additional lab partners to try things out on.

I gave each player my absolute attention. Whatever drill I came up with, however we spent the hour or so, my goal was broader than any specific skill: I wanted them to feel empowered when they left the gym. I figured if they could consistently handle the complexity, intensity, and pace of the workouts I dreamt up, then practice and games would feel like Oreos soaked in milk. I hoped that afterward they would hear my voice, remember our lessons, and tap into their own well of inspiration.

This meant knowing more than the game. It meant knowing the pressures they felt in and around it. All those years I spent on the playground sped up my learning curve, but my desire to understand and help them meant I had to learn the culture of high-profile basketball players. Let's face it, NBA players and soon-to-be NBA players are young, fit, and famous in their world, so their tastes in music, clothes, language, outlook, interests, and circle of friends differed from mine. Over time I learned from them what they considered the hottest artist; the most current dances and slang; the best lyrics; the latest clothing trends; the "in" restaurants, lounges, and nightclubs; the names of the prettiest women in the magazines and videos; the power brokers in business, in sports, and on the streets; and all the relevant gossip in music and sports. Imagine the importance when doing business in Korea of knowing the intricacies of Korean culture; the same idea applied here.

These players trusted me with developing their game; only family and health were higher priorities for them. They invested so much energy and effort in chasing their NBA dreams, and had so much of their happiness, identity, and self-esteem built around their determination to make it happen. I treasured their trust, and I was absolutely committed to doing my best to help them get there.

Time was scarce for me with a full-time law gig, so I carved out patches of my evenings and weekends, and even left the office early on occasion though I was well aware this could cost me my job. It was a good job, but the training sessions felt like the thing I was always intended to do.

Living in the Washington, DC, area, I naturally saw a lot of the basketball program at the University of Maryland, my alma mater. During the summer of 2000, Steve Francis introduced me to junior guard Juan Dixon; Juan and I spoke briefly and exchanged contact information, but I didn't expect to hear from Juan immediately. High-profile athletes are often wary of forging new relationships because they assume outsiders want a slice of their magic. In a sports world filled with snake charmers and aggressive salesmen, I prefer to develop rapport patiently and grow relationships organically.

I ran into Juan a few weeks later while in the gym with Steve. With one eye on Steve and the other on Juan, I noticed how Juan ran for the first time. From his stride, I suspected he had one leg longer than the other. His guide hand moved whenever he released the ball, which affects the ball rotation and the consistency of his release—something I first discovered when I taught myself how to shoot. He dribbled the ball so close to his leg on his pull-up jumper that defenders could easily swipe the ball from him; I'd struggled with that as a small player up against taller and longer defenders. He played on his heels rather than the balls of his feet, which left him off-balance both on defense and on offense. He stared at the floor when he dribbled, so he could not see his teammates or defenders. His movement patterns and inefficiency with the ball stood out to me immediately, like a lime-green miniskirt at a Hasidic wedding. I didn't comment or offer Juan any suggestions. I figured he'd let me know when he was ready.

Juan eventually scheduled a session with me later in the week. I came directly from the office and changed my clothes while standing behind several large wrestling mats in the back corner of the gym. In my brief time with him I'd noticed he was animated and hyper, pacing back and forth while we spoke. Everyone processes information differently, so with Juan I decided the less dialogue the better. I demonstrated a drill slowly, which he then attempted to mirror, increasing his speed with each repetition. I manipulated his feet, legs, arms, hands, and torso so he could see and feel what I considered proper movement patterns and mechanics.

I tapped his guide hand when it moved during the release of his jump shot. I tapped his chin to force his head upward when he glanced at the floor while exploding forward with a left-hand dribble. He was startled because I had invaded his personal space, but the tapping sensations were necessary to remind him of his mechanics. I repeated myself multiple times and with a different inflection so Juan would hear my voice even when I wasn't with him. This was something I'd learned from a California Bar exam instructor whose awkward way of speaking actually helped me remember massive amounts of information.

I knew that at the highest levels of the game he'd face defenders who were not only athletic but *long*—with great reach. He'd have to create space for his pull-up jumper, and the way to do that was to dribble out, at a forty-five-degree angle away from his body, pushing the ball past the defender's outside shoulder and using his quickness to get by; the opponent could still reach for it, but now he'd be hitting Juan's shoulder instead of the ball, committing a foul in the process. You're faster when you run than when you dribble, so I recommended he push the ball out and take multiple steps to retrieve it.

I made sure to ask for his feedback, because encouraging his voice would help him see his development as collaborative. "How are you feeling? Is this uncomfortable? Is it starting to feel more natural? Can you see how this would work in real life?"

In less than an hour he was already tired and started reverting to his old habits: head down, guide hand shifting, too many dribbles in the same place. I cut the workout short because I wanted him to retain the proper mechanics; it was better for him to stop there than to reinforce his bad habits when fatigued. When a player can only think about catching his breath, his movements are more intuitive because he has no focus to give them—this is an important benchmark in the learning process, one I watch for constantly. If you can perform correctly with me when you're fatigued, game conditions will be easy because you'll never be as tired in a game as you are in our practices.

After our session, he asked for our schedule for the remainder of the summer. That was his assurance he loved the game. That was what I longed to hear.

For the rest of the summer we met in the evenings as often as we could. I left work early for the long commute to the gym—a forty-minute subway ride followed by a thirty-minute drive. I hoped I could catch up on my billable hours on weekends and early mornings before my colleagues arrived.

Efficiency and *space* were our watchwords. Throughout the summer he had exceptional focus and great energy no matter where and when we met. He was never sluggish. He never had off days. He ran hard, played hard, practiced hard, thought hard, focused hard, and tried hard. He was relentless, as if he were playing for something bigger than just an NBA dream.

We spent hundreds of hours together in the gym, and I saw many layers to his personality. He was meticulous with appearance and hygiene. He managed to indulge every couple of weeks in inexpensive pedicures, manicures, and haircuts. On occasion I'd give him a lift to his off-campus apartment when he didn't have use of his girlfriend's car; his impeccably organized room reminded me of a hotel room recently serviced by housekeeping. He kept his shoes spotless and stacked in their original boxes. He ironed his clothes precisely, folding them neatly and hanging them in his closets. His outfits matched, even when he trained. Like many people who don't own much, he valued the things he did own, treating his personal property with the pride of a homeowner. A psychologist might diagnose Juan as obsessive-compulsive, but I thought he showed great appreciation for what he had. His attention to detail helped him become systematic and conscientious in his approach to basketball. I hoped it would eventually translate to his life in general.

His junior season was scheduled to begin in October, and I reminded him to chase personal goals when he trained on his own and to focus on team goals at practice and while with his team. Throughout the season, he called me often to report on his progress. "I killed it" was how he would describe his great practices.

Forget drugs—the high from self-improvement is legendary and has its own community of addicts. They want more once they taste it and feel its effects. Juan transformed himself into one of the country's best players. The extra work and the success it brought him made him even hungrier. Love, effort, and commitment brought him closer to things that mattered to him. He sacrificed more than anyone else, and as a result he began to resent the lazy. He wouldn't let anyone snatch bread off his plate.

His brilliant junior season came to an abrupt end when Maryland lost to Duke in the national semifinals: Maryland's first-ever trip to the Final Four. Afterward, he called me to vent. He felt he'd let himself and his team down. While his teammates took time off after the long season, Juan shook loose from his sadness and returned to the gym with even more intensity and focus. He had a remarkable ability to close chapters in his life and move forward.

That summer he listed his goals as winning ACC Player of the Year and a national championship, and becoming a first-round NBA draft pick. I never doubted Juan. He treated his goals with such sanctity, as if he had a handshake deal with God. Without hesitation, I made myself available to him again. He had become like a younger brother to me, and I lived vicariously through his success.

I learned a lot from and about Juan during all the time we spent together sitting on a wrestling mat in a quiet gym. He shared with me his dreams, struggles, family, student life, and childhood. Juan had a few prominent tattoos on his chest and arms that told about his life, but he hadn't yet shared all these stories with me. Over the previous year I'd discovered from one of his teammates that Juan had endured unimaginable tragedy. He never talked about it and neither did I.

That changed one evening during the early spring of his senior year.

"It's going to be crazy on senior night," he said. "I don't know what I'm goin' to do. What if I cry?"

Why would you cry? I thought but didn't say anything.

"I'm not goin' to have my parents walk me to center court," he added as he wiped the tears from his cheeks with his hands.

For the first time in our two years, he opened up about his background. His mother and father had both abused drugs and died from AIDS-related complications when he was a teenager—an incredibly tragic story too cruel for a child to imagine or experience.

I didn't know what to say, so I said nothing, just listened.

"I'm sure my brother will be there," he added. "You comin'?"

"Of course, man," I said.

He sat up and gave me a hug.

Senior night came, and was followed by an exceptional run through the postseason. Juan earned All-Conference honors, was a consensus All-American, and was named Conference Player of the Year. He led Maryland to the national championship and was named Most Outstanding Player at the Final Four.

After the national championship game, I met him at his team hotel in Atlanta. He had cut a portion of the net from the championship game and wore it proudly around his neck. He hugged me immediately when he saw me, then led me to a banquet room to avoid reporters and camera crews. He began to pace.

"We did it, man. We did it. Me and you, we did it," he sobbed, tears streaming down his face.

He collapsed in my arms. He thanked me, but he had no idea how much I wanted to thank him. Sometimes we meet someone who affects us and teaches us something about ourselves. I was struggling to find happiness in my life as a lawyer, becoming cynical and melancholy. I complained and prayed for an answer. Yet I watched Juan chase a dream with no certainty and live life with incredible optimism despite suffering tragedy no young person should know. He pushed down as hard as he could on the accelerator to make sure he lived without regrets. He never complained and he laughed all the time. He inspired me to see life much differently, to be courageous in my pursuits, and to not look outwardly for answers when sometimes there really weren't any to be found.

CHAPTER NINE

MAKING VARSITY

mom knows best
#usually

From working with Steve Francis and Juan Dixon, word of my sessions spread, and soon they resembled a U of Maryland practice, with Juan, Steve Blake, Lonny Baxter, and Drew Nicholas all attending and working their asses off. A few pros who lived in the area began showing up as well, and I was always happy to help anyone I could.

A couple of years after I started training players, I was having lunch with my mom.

"How's work?" she asked in Hebrew.

"You mean law?" I replied.

"Yes."

"Sucks as usual."

"How about basketball?" she added.

"It's cool. Enjoying it."

"You spend a lot of time working with them."

"Absolutely, it takes up a lot of my time."

"It is several hours each time, considering your travel to and from them, and then the time spent working with them and talking with them," she continued in Hebrew.

"Not to mention all the phone calls and texts throughout the day." I laughed.

"How much do you charge these guys?" she asked sternly.

Her question caught me off guard. I paused. I felt embarrassed.

"I don't," I finally said. "How could I charge them?"

"In their eyes, you're only worth what they are willing to pay for you," she added.

I wanted to argue, but I couldn't. She was right.

Over the course of my professional career, I had earned a living doing something I hated. How could I now earn a living doing what I loved? How could I charge someone for something I was willing to do for free? I didn't know how to quantify or monetize my services. I didn't know anyone who did what I did. An agent had once given me some pocket money for preparing his player for the draft, but that was early on and I just took what he gave me. There was no industry standard to help me approximate a figure.

Lastly, I didn't know how to raise the question directly with the few pro players I worked with. I was afraid to disturb something that seemed fragile because it was built on trust. What if I offended or alienated them, and I lost the opportunity to do this thing that gave me so much joy?

My mom's words echoed like a siren signaling an impending tornado. I came to the office the next day still rattled by her question. She was absolutely right, but I didn't have an answer. In the meantime, I continued to work at the firm and volunteer my time with the players. Eventually I would have to receive some sort of compensation for all my work. I was helping players live their NBA dreams and earn generations' worth of money. In between their agent, manager, financial advisor, insurance broker, personal chef, private security guard, and publicist, there had to be some room for me somewhere on the payroll.

I thought, *Fuck, the last thing I want them to think is that now it's all about the money.*

I pictured them looking disgusted and saying, *I thought you cared.* I heard those words over and over in my head.

I did care, I always cared, and I always will care. But I had student loans to pay, groceries to buy, bills to address, and, like the players, I wanted to help my family financially.

And so I thought, a lot, for quite a while. Most of the thoughts were internal pep talks to convince myself it was time to get paid for my work. I reminded myself about the contract negotiations that happen between players and teams. Like me, the players were doing what they love, playing a game they had played for free up until at least the age of eighteen. At that point, whether it was by declaring for the NBA out of high school, as college underclassmen, or upon graduation, they matured as players and could now command a salary for their work. My situation really wasn't so different. I volunteered in the beginning as I learned the ropes and honed my craft. Over a couple of years I had improved the quality of my work product and developed a service that benefited the athlete. They made the transition from college to the pros, and now it was my turn to go from volunteer to business owner. Besides, for this to work, we both had to invest in the process. To be its best, our partnership really ought to be mutually beneficial.

A few months later, the phone rang in my office at work. A senior partner's extension showed up on the caller ID.

Strange, I thought. *He had never called me before.* I picked up the phone and he asked me to come to his office, which was only a few doors away from mine. I knocked.

"Come on in."

I took a seat.

"How are you?" he asked.

"Good. Um, what's up?" I asked.

"First and foremost, we've all been pleased with your work and really enjoy having you here," he said.

I knew immediately where this conversation was headed.

He began to deliver the bad news while nibbling on the stash of baby carrots he always kept on his desk. "The firm is going in a different direction. But please know we aren't rushing you out of here immediately. You will still be paid for another three months and this will give you some time to start looking for other work. And if there is anything you need, like a letter of recommendation or a contact, please do not hesitate to let me know." He said it all calmly, as if he had delivered this speech many times before.

You don't know NBA commissioner David Stern, do you? I thought.

I left the office early that day. It was a strange day. I felt anxious, yet somehow relieved. The following day was even stranger. Whether you resign or get fired, it doesn't really hit you until the following morning when you realize there are no immediate consequences for hitting the snooze button.

While I liked my colleagues and the firm had treated me very well over the last few years, I never lost the feeling that I didn't want to practice law. Maybe the layoff made a decision for me that I didn't have the courage yet to make on my own.

I didn't know where I would turn next.

Fortunately, I believed in faith more than I did dreams. I could see dreams when I closed my eyes, but I couldn't see this dream because I didn't know what I wanted. Meanwhile faith required me to believe things would be better just beyond the horizon.

In the meantime, I had recently connected with someone I

knew from playing ball as a teenager. A company he founded owned several online properties, and he was looking for investors. I was still living with my parents and had some money put away from my law job, and now I also had some time I could devote to helping this start-up grow.

And I thought a lot about my mom's words, in the context of faith. I needed to have faith that I would have the courage to talk with the players about payment; faith this delicate conversation would not shatter my relationships with them; faith I would not forsake what made me happy in the name of a dollar; faith the players cared for me as much as I did for them; faith I helped them with something they considered so precious; faith the heavens would not abandon me when I worried; and faith the game would continue to transport me somewhere amazing.

A few months after leaving the law firm I received a call from Elton Brand, who at the time played for the Los Angeles Clippers. He was scheduled to be in DC for a few days, and he wanted to set up some training. I met Elton years earlier when he attended a few workouts with Steve Francis prior to the 1999 NBA draft, where he was the number-one pick.

We met at the home of a friend, a dot-com millionaire who'd built a full-court gym inside his house. It was private, secure, and exclusive—important buzzwords for the high-profile athlete. Besides, the venue would let players rub elbows with someone who had more money than they did and who wanted nothing in return. The eight- and nine-figure boys' club was exclusive and created camaraderie and respect among its members.

Whether it was our first training session or our hundredth, my excitement never waned. Elton was cerebral, thoughtful in his approach, and meticulous with his preparation. We spent that morning working on his conditioning and his low-postgame using medicine balls and weighted basketballs. There was so much I still didn't know about training and the NBA, so I welcomed Elton's considerable insights and suggestions. Drills had to have context, and since he knew his team's offensive and defensive principles inside and out, we kept within those parameters while we trained. Elton left the workouts feeling fatigued, challenged, engaged, and improved. Everything went well, but I still didn't have the nerve to say anything to Elton about compensation.

Once the season started, he asked whether I could travel to Los Angeles to work with him. He had missed about a month of games due to a hairline fracture in his foot, and the doctors had recently cleared him to begin his on-court training. He wanted to spend some time with me before resuming practice with his team. Before I left for Los Angeles, we spoke by phone to coordinate logistics. In the middle of our conversation, I finally mustered my courage and mumbled, "Pay whatever you want." I didn't know if he even heard me, because I said it so fast and tried to disguise it by inserting it at the end of a long sentence. The whatever-it's-worth-to-you model came to me because I couldn't come up with a figure. How do you put a price on what you love? He could have paid me with a bag of jelly beans and I still would have done it.

When I arrived in Los Angeles, Elton met me at a beautiful hotel in Marina del Rey. He gave me a man hug. He handed the front desk his credit card, paying for my room. He then handed me a white envelope.

"It's your per diem," he said.

I paused. "Thanks, EB."

I unpacked my bags and left the white envelope on the hotel bed. Every few minutes I glanced at it. I waited an hour before I peeled it open, wondering if Elton would have a change of heart. I didn't want to return him an opened envelope.

Soon after, I received a check from Elton. I couldn't believe what had just happened. One of the best players in the world had just paid me to do what I loved, what I had done for free only minutes ago.

Throughout my life, I was brainwashed to believe work was supposed to feel impossible, as much of a struggle as if I'd been hired to build the Great Wall of China alone and in time for Hanukkah. Work was supposed to overwhelm you, fatigue you, stress you. Training athletes never felt like any of this.

I contributed to something they considered as precious as I did, and now I was getting paid for it. And it didn't change anything either, not for me or the players I worked with. In fact, it strengthened the dynamic of our relationship because it added another layer of respect. We respected each other's time, craft, efforts, and the importance each held in our lives.

And for several years thereafter, I had my mom deposit the checks I received from the players, to reassure her I'd heeded her advice and had even discovered a way to earn a living doing what I loved most.

CHAPTER TEN

TRAINING DAYS

never underestimate the passionate man,
even without hands he can still create a picasso
#selfreliant #creative #resourceful

There's an old joke about how becoming a writer is like becoming a prostitute: First you do it for love, then you do it for a few friends, and finally you do it for money. You could say the same thing about the path I had taken to being a professional trainer, though I never lost the love and still haven't.

With Elton Brand marking my transition to being a full-fledged professional, I had decisions to make about how I wanted to conduct my business. To begin with, slacks, ties, dress shirts, memos, research, and meetings were no longer a part of my life. I didn't have a facility of my own, and I didn't want one; I also didn't want any employees, business cards, or partnerships. If I could develop my game with just a ball and a rim, then why couldn't my guys?

I envisioned a minimalist approach with little capital expenditure, great service, and happy clients. I was already putting some of my philosophy into practice with the athletes I trained so far. I suspected my approach worked because the players improved, felt empowered, and even shared my gospel with their peers.

I usually train players in modest, nondescript gyms with no audience, using a few worn basketballs, jump ropes, cones, and a stopwatch. I want them to work intensely and purposefully in an environment that emphasizes efficiency and accountability. Water breaks are short and when needed. I emphasize self-reliance; I never want to hear the word *politics* used as a reason for mediocre performance.

Instruction comes in bursts of dialogue and demonstration, recognizing that athletes—being people of action—tend to have short attention spans. I engage their competitive nature and challenge their stamina by keeping score in shooting drills: plus one for a make and minus one for a miss, until they reach whatever score we designate that day, such as plus seven. That's at least seven more makes than misses, which can take a long time when you're already fatigued. Imagine, after thirty minutes with heavy conditioning integrated into every drill, and now it's time for dessert: shooting, drizzled with sprints. Legs, shoulders, forearms, and lungs feel like they've been pierced by shrapnel caused by the combustion from earlier drills demanding quickness, agility, speed, power, balance, and skill. You finally get to shoot, and you miss, miss again, and then miss again. Now you're worried, your confidence shaken as you realize you're down to minus three, anticipating this could last awhile if you don't connect on ten consecutive shots to reach plus seven, with the consequence being even more conditioning that you've convinced yourself you can't handle at that moment. As you fight your way through the fatigue and the challenge, you notice your peers on the sideline, watching and encouraging you as they try to keep their thoughts away from their own nervous anticipation. This system creates accountability and focus. I don't just encourage a make; I want to highlight the miss, because it reflects an opportunity for the player to self-diagnose and recalibrate his focus, mechanics, and rhythm.

The gyms aren't sexy, the equipment isn't the latest and greatest, and water comes from fountains, not bottled and stocked in refrigerators alongside the energy drinks. We strip the game to its rawest form, so players can see the game the way we did as children: playing in the park; shooting baskets on rainy days; dribbling on snow-covered payment until we couldn't feel our fingers; running full-court sprints on a rain-covered blacktop; layering our T-shirts and wearing hoodies to avoid the bulky winter coat even on the coldest day; waking up every day with basketball on our minds.

I create a deliberately barren environment to remove the excesses many players associate with the game—the rewards instead of the satisfaction. I want them to reconnect with basketball on a primal, gut level: Think Rocky Balboa pummeling carcasses in frozen meat lockers until the skin on his fingers was raw and bloodied. I want them to remember they play because they love the game, not for all the crap that comes with it. If they don't, they'll have a short career and then give way to somebody who cares more.

If I was going to maximize their ability, emphasize self-reliance, and restore their love for the game, I had to thoroughly understand the psyche of any athlete I trained. They weren't always the most eloquent when I asked how they were feeling, so I listened for the tone and inflection in their voice, the cadence in their words, their breathing, and their choice in topics of conversation. I watched their gait and posture to gauge their mood. I stood close to them so I could smell whether they had liquor on their breath from the night before. I noticed whether they matched their sneakers with their apparel, how quickly they laced their shoes, whether they followed their warm-up protocol. I kept track of how often I had to repeat instructions to them.

All these observations helped me tailor our training sessions to my reading of a player's mood. Some days I can just tell when a guy is energized, and some days when he's lethargic. When they open the gym doors and immediately share with me their escapades from the night before, that's a sign. When they take an unreasonably long time to switch from flip-flops to basketball sneakers? A sign. When the first thing they do is lean their backside against the wall to assist them with their gradual descent to the floor as if they have arthritic knees at age twenty-two, and then they check all their different phones—"hold on, E; hold on, E, one sec . . ."—I know they're not feeling it that day. Maybe that's a day when we'll go lighter physically, but with a lot of dialogue to get at the reason for their lack of focus. You'll never hear me toss insults at them. I don't micromanage their lives. I roll with it, because some days they just don't have it—like all of us. Meanwhile, I hope they'll learn through experience that the more mentally and physically engaged they are, the more productive our sessions become.

On the other hand, some days they burst into the gym feeling inspired. They may have watched a highlight reel or YouTube clips of a game they dominated, or replayed in their head our conversation about their All-Star potential, or spent time celebrating their son's birthday and that gave them a renewed sense of focus, or spoke with their agent about a potential big contract for next season, or maybe even played particularly well in an off-season pickup game against a franchise player from another team, so they realize they're close to becoming really good. Those are the days when we train even more intensely, often until they feel overwhelmed, which is an important step in the learning process. It helps tone down their expectations and arrogance by highlighting the distance between good and great. Either way, long routine or short, their effort represents an homage to the ways in which their lives have been blessed.

These details give me context for their workouts, but more

important, they tell me that player's story. I want them to long for greatness, because I know I do. Greatness is a way of life, a direction. Every NBA player is remarkably talented, with a stellar résumé and physical gifts. But it takes much more than that to find the degree of success they hope for. I have to learn whether they want to be great, and if they do, I encourage them to become absolutely ferocious in their quest for greatness.

Would he play even without a paycheck or applause? I wonder, so I listen to their tone of voice and watch their eyes at the end of a workout to see if they're eager to hit rewind and return to the gym the following day. If they are, then "it's on," as my guys say. When I know they care as much as I do, I anticipate their phone calls, texts, e-mails, and instant messages at all hours, for any reason at all: to schedule additional workouts, ask for advice, get feedback on anything they think might matter in their pursuit of greatness. My message is clear: Love what you do, not the material gifts that come with it. And if you don't, don't fake it, just find something else that you do love.

At the same time, it's up to me to keep these exceptional athletes involved and engaged. Stamina matters, physical and mental, and it's an important ingredient in the pursuit of greatness. Hard work doesn't come with guarantees of success; it takes mental stamina for a player to have faith and persevere with focus even when he can't see the finish line. Improved physical stamina follows when he applies the necessary work ethic and discipline; the ability to push hard for forty-eight minutes in game conditions is a component of every aspect of his performance, and as his capacity expands, so do his opportunities for learning.

But conditioning doesn't just happen in pro sports. NBA players don't respond well when you demand they "touch lines"—sprints that require them to bend down and touch the baseline and/or the foul line and/or the midcourt line before they turn and sprint back. Boring, right? So instead I make sure the conditioning drills include activities that develop their technique, done in ways that interest them, make sense to them, and challenge them. It could involve a ball in their hand, making precise cuts—doing things that resemble the movements they would use in practice and in games. It's all in a basketball context, and they can see the incremental benefits each day as they play pickup against one another in competitive drills during our sessions. And then—voilà—they'll fight through the fatigue because they recognize it's only temporary and it's directly related to their improvement. That's when the real workout begins.

Anyone can fatigue anybody; in ten minutes I can make anyone throw up by forcing them to run faster and harder. This kind of conditioning has some indirect benefit to the player, but he will improve more and faster with performance-based conditioning that incorporates technical skill in a gamelike context. There has to be a purpose. Always. Basketball stars on this level will not just run to run.

I do all this without raising my voice at my athletes. I have no intention of being a martinet or a tyrant. I don't understand why it's acceptable in sports to yell and curse at players, because ultimately a coach and a player are in something resembling an employer-employee relationship. You don't yell and scream at your employees when you work at Apple—unless you founded the company and you're a genius—so why is it OK when you work for a sports team? You even see it on the high school and college level, this culture of fear, which I consider counterproductive and inhibiting. When people describe a coach's tantrum as "tough love," I think they and the coach are wrong and even insane. Can you imagine tossing a chair across a conference room? A complaint would be filed, human resources would be called, and you would be out of a job faster than the autocorrect on your iPhone.

I keep the sessions closed because I believe that you have to feel comfortable to feel creative. People don't generally respond well to judgment, criticism, and fear. The best results come when the athletes are calm, and I encourage their mistakes. Imagine making those same mistakes around a front office and the coaching staff—the people who control your paycheck and minutes. You would certainly feel reluctant to try something new that might expose your weaknesses. Ever wonder why they prefer to do what they already do well rather than work on what they don't? Pro sports have become a business of highlighting what's wrong with players rather than what's right. It's better just to pretend the eyeballs don't exist. Play for *you*.

And then after the workout's over and they're tired, that's the best time to get to know them. Their defenses are down, and we've just been through something together. I can listen to them and find out what they want and how they got here. I want to know where they came from and how they learn, and that's not something they can tell you in an answer to a direct question. I work best with them and help them the most if I can see the world through their eyes. These guys are not stupid or inarticulate; whatever language they speak, they speak it very well, and it isn't all in the words. It's not incumbent on them to understand me; it's up to me to understand them.

I wasn't following a formula or a model when I started figuring this out. Years later, I'm still improvising and learning. For the most part I've simply trusted my intuition and my instincts, and I know it's working when I see the players improve and return eagerly for more.

My way isn't the only way.

"Idan, you guys still working out at six A.M.?" Russell Westbrook asks me with a smile.

Some players think my sessions are too tough, and according to Melo, "Most players don't really want to work that hard. That's why you don't work with a hundred guys."

It has to be a good fit.

Some guys want to do only what they do well, others prefer

to train conventionally, and others just maintain—that's why they train at civilian gyms or with friends, or at luxury facilities that resemble country clubs, where they can play video games and indulge in flat-screen TVs, private lockers, and lounges for napping. That's not my way. I want you in and I want you out, real efficient, serious, and no bullshit.

CHAPTER ELEVEN

THE POINT

it will take as long as it takes. u'll know when you're done
#notimetable

In the spring of 2005 I spent some time in the gym with sophomore guard Chris Paul, an All-American from Wake Forest, prior to the NBA draft. His agents allowed him to select the trainer for his pre-draft preparation; agents are often afraid to alienate their clients, so they give them options. Putting the choice in the college kid's hands helps the agent hedge his risk and deflect blame if things don't go as well as expected on draft day.

After our first workout Chris and his brother told his DC-based agents that he wanted to remain in the city to train with me. His agents were relieved he chose to stay in town so they could forge a stronger relationship with him. But I sensed their reluctance to entrust his development to someone who in their eyes did not look the part. On our first day, they watched Chris run through a battery of shooting, ball-handling, and conditioning drills while he listened to my brief instruction. If life mimicked comic books, the thought bubble over their heads would read, *I can do what he's doing; he's just passing him the ball and telling him where to run. What's the big deal?* I wish it were that easy.

During our first week of pre-draft training, the nerves and excitement were more potent than a case of Red Bull. Imagine that the one thing you've been obsessed with your entire life is going to be yours very soon. This would turn even the laziest man into a laborer and the most jaded cynic into a believer. But Chris's nervous energy wore off soon enough as fatigue set in.

It was understandable that he'd be tired. He'd spent several weeks traveling, accepting awards, and making decisions about the next chapters in his life. He'd selected an agent, withdrawn from Wake Forest before the end of his sophomore year, and relocated to DC to prepare for the draft. He had a tough schedule: 6:00 A.M. wake-up call, on the court from 7:00 A.M. to 9:00 A.M., resistance training in the late morning, lunch, nap, stretch—and then, when possible, back at the gym in the late afternoon.

At first Chris thought he would prepare with me for his team workouts prior to the draft. The teams call in the players they're interested in, to evaluate them and to measure their body fat, their length, their height, their weight. They test their flexibility, power, strength and agility, quickness, and anaerobic endurance. To test his basketball skills, they might put a player through a number of different sequences to see how fast he learns an offensive play, run him through a pick-and-roll scheme, then maybe play him two-on-two and three-on-three with other players to see if he's competitive. They'll have the players take stationary shots at different spots on the court, college-range threes, NBA threes. Ultimately, the players I work with prior to the draft say those team workouts are very, very easy for them. I tell guys I'm not preparing them for the draft, I'm preparing them for two days after—the start of summer-league practices, and then training camp and the regular season. That's why the level of intensity is so great and I demand so much more of them than they need just to get through the draft process.

There were no pat-on-the-back life clichés and pep talks. Sessions were intentionally difficult and focused on making Chris a more refined and efficient player. I tried to build on his strengths and highlight his weaknesses with unconventional drills, like reacting with defensive slides to the tennis balls I would toss at him. Over time he would feel empowered as he learned to conquer the unreasonable.

I insisted Chris train alone, and we maintained that regimen for as long as we needed to. I suspected this would cause him to struggle with the pace and intensity of our workouts, which was good because he would begin to feel vulnerable. Vulnerability meant he'd be more inclined to acknowledge whatever weakness he kept locked inside his thoughts, which I hoped would both motivate him and connect him with his love of the game and his desire for greatness.

At first, his conditioning was only fair, so I incorporated a sprint or quick movement into every drill. Training one-on-one eliminated rest breaks between sets, challenged his endurance, and would ultimately improve his conditioning. If he could handle these sessions alone, then any audition for an NBA team—or any practice and game he would play—would be as easy as Jay Z going platinum on his next album.

I wanted him to become more efficient with the ball and give purpose to each dribble. I created drills that required him to go baseline to baseline, offense to defense, and back again, shuttling to every position on the floor in a finite amount of time. This helped him to shrink the court by learning to cover ground faster and with fewer dribbles.

We worked on his lateral movement, essential to playing the game east and west as well as north and south. Too many basketball experts hammer the idea that you've got to go north-south, always toward the basket. Yes, attacking the basket often gets you a better shot, but basketball's a game played in many different directions: back and forth, side to side, at a variety of angles. On offense, it reminds me of the games of tag we played as kids: You have to elude a defender, and you can't do that by always pressing forward.

I showed Chris how to dribble while taking a series of lateral steps, not crossing his feet. This keeps his shoulders square to the basket, so that he can move sideways and still square up for a jump shot at any time, while maintaining his ability to shift direction and get free of the defense or run the defender into a ball screen. It was like learning a dance step, awkward at first until he learned the rhythm behind it, but he became so good at it that he could play the game in multiple planes of motion, making him almost impossible to stop.

I never belittled Chris when he struggled; I never ridiculed or cursed at him or any athlete in our sessions. I never questioned Chris's effort; in fact, I usually gave him the option of doing less. He was self-motivated, complex, competitive, and self-reliant, so I assumed he would select the tougher alternative when it was made available to him.

These traits were a by-product of his childhood. Chris was raised by a wonderful family in a loving support system that placed God and family above all else. Religion, family, love, spirituality, and faith all found a way to intersect with his love for the game, and I would have been irresponsible to ignore this when we worked together. I don't like having someone else in the gym when I'm working with a player—but Chris's brother was his best friend and had moved with Chris from Winston-Salem to DC to help him make the transition, so if Chris wanted his brother at the workouts, then his brother attended

the workouts. Acknowledging his value system, giving him me-
thodical reminders and positive reinforcement—these things
were as important as his physical training and would keep him
steady through any stressful and unfamiliar times he might face.

We also spent a lot of time talking and texting. The conversations often took a serious tone because I hoped he would prepare mentally for the demands of NBA life. We talked about
jealous veterans, hypersensitive media, overbearing coaches, impatient front office personnel, commission-starved agents, long
road trips, disingenuous women, and fickle fans. The NBA isn't
a league filled with patience, hugs, and kisses. He would have to
find ways to keep his edge despite the newfound opulence, luxury, and freedom. Chris didn't need any help preparing for the
NBA draft; he was taken by New Orleans with the fourth pick
of the first round, and he was going to be a top pick even if he
did nothing but eat Krispy Kreme donuts and drink Mountain
Dew all spring. But success in the NBA starts before the draft,
and Chris's ability and dedication set that bar especially high. I
reminded him regularly of the goals I knew he could achieve:
Rookie of the Year, All-Star Games, NBA playoffs, Olympics, a
gold medal, and league MVP.

One afternoon I received a call from Chris's agent at the
time, saying an NBA general manager wanted to informally observe Chris working out because his team had a high draft pick. I
reluctantly agreed. I called Gilbert Arenas, who then played for
the Washington Wizards. I mentioned to Gil I was preparing
Chris for the draft and I invited him to train with Chris. Gil
didn't watch much college basketball, so he wasn't familiar with
Chris's game, but he did want to resume his off-season workouts.

I surprised Chris when I arrived with Gil one Saturday
morning. He would finally have the chance to train with another player. Gil was an NBA superstar, so everyone knew him,
but I still introduced Chris, his brother, and his agent to Gil. I
wanted to make this unusual situation as normal as I could.

The session began with a few shooting drills and some light conditioning. Chris knew the steps, so he went first. Gil followed. After thirty minutes, I organized some competitive drills. Chris and Gil would play five games of one-on-one, game to five. Each one-on-one game started on a different spot on the court, with a particular instruction—for example, at the top of the key with the offensive player facing the basket, or on the wing with his back to the hoop. Defensive deflections and missed shots would cause a change of possession. At the end of the first game, Gil glanced at me quickly and mouthed, *He's goin' to be a muthafucka.*

Chris won the first game, the second game, the third game, the fourth game, and the fifth game. In Gil's defense, this was just a game of one-on-one, played at the beginning of the NBA off-season, and Gil hadn't picked up a ball since the end of the season. Nevertheless, Gil still a top player in the league at that time and Chris more than held his own. Chris was excited. He now knew he belonged in the league. Seeing his performance reaffirmed what I originally thought: He was special, and I finally could see in color and in detail how special he really would become.

Afterward, I introduced myself to the GM and asked him what he thought about Chris. He said he thought Chris was good.

"That's it? Just good?" I asked. How could he not see his gift?

"He was OK."

"Did you not watch the last hour? He is more than good. He will be great."

"He was OK," he repeated.

I couldn't believe it. If I had had a microphone at that moment, I would have yelled at the top of my lungs, *Chris Paul will become one of the fifteen greatest players in the history of the NBA.*

OK? OK???? Maybe he was just being noncommittal, but there is no way anyone watching could have used those two letters to describe what we had just seen. Impossible. This was when Gilbert Arenas was healthy, when Gilbert Arenas was a top-five player in the world, when Gilbert Arenas was putting up multiple forty-point games—and this kid just dismantled him: a kid who only weeks earlier had completed his sophomore season at Wake. That was extraordinary.

I thought, *Did he not see what I just saw? Could he really not feel the same excitement I just felt?*

NBA owners spend millions of dollars on scouting budgets run by supposedly top basketball minds. This GM had just witnessed something truly special and he was debating whether the guards on his current roster were better than Chris. The obvious is sometimes the hardest to see.

As Chris's career has progressed, he's achieved many of the goals we talked about—Rookie of the Year, first team All-NBA, first team All-Defensive team, two Olympic gold medals. He's led the league in assists and steals—total and per-game—and has finished in the top five of the MVP voting four times so far. He is without question the top point guard of his generation.

He takes his leadership role seriously, on and off the court. He's a responsible father, husband, son, brother, friend, and philanthropist. He coaches AAU basketball in the off-season, giving back to the game by passing along the knowledge he's gained through his struggles, diligence, commitment, and experience.

If you ever have the chance to meet Chris, you'll be surprised that he can be so dominant a player while being such a normal height and size. In order to play in the NBA as a regular-size person, you have to become quick and fast, but you also have to become comfortable with contact—finding it and taking it. I created a few drills for Chris to acclimate him to the contact he faces in every game, the pushing and slapping he can expect from defenders. I created the dribbling sled drill that has been copied in some Under Armour and Gatorade commercials, where a player dribbles the ball while someone stands in front of him pushing against his shoulders like a football sled. I've spent many hours taking this stance against Chris, trying to limit his movement as he fights against me. I want him to become a bully during our drills, to move as if there is no barrier while at the same time focusing on his handle, power, and strength.

This sled drill when it's done right serves an additional purpose. Basketball requires a defensive stance, but spending an extended period of time in that stance can cause tightness in the hips. The pushing motion against the "sled" requires a knee drive that also strengthens and increases the range of motion in the hip. It improves a player's leverage when his foot strikes and pushes off the ground, which helps with speed and power. I then integrated a ball-handling and sensory component to complement the drill.

During some of our stationary ball-handling drills I would slap at his forearms and even grab and hold his arm as he struggled to move his wrist forward. The game can be brutal at times, and referees can't catch every grab, push, or smack. Chris learned how to absorb this kind of contact without compromising the ball, giving him another edge.

With his ability to score and to move effectively and efficiently on the court, Chris creates opportunities for his teammates that other point guards can't. Think of it like being a quarterback in the NFL: If you have a great line in front of you, and you can stand in the pocket as long as you want, eventually someone is going to break into the open and you'll see him. Because Chris is so good with the ball, moving and controlling and not giving up his dribble, he can extend plays deep enough into the shot clock that he'll eventually find an opening for the pass or shot. It's as though his remarkable abilities give him extra time in each possession.

As the years have gone by, we haven't worked together as

much as we did at the start. He has many interests and carries an enormous load. When we have gotten together, I've always respected his time and tried to maximize the intensity, functionality, and efficiency of our sessions—which usually took place in the early morning hours, before most people have hit snooze or taken their first sip of coffee.

I promised him when we first met that I would do everything I could to help him. I fully expect to be there for his Hall of Fame induction speech one day.

CHAPTER TWELVE

THE REAL CARMELO

it made 4 better reading once we removed the cover
#get2knowhimb4ujudgehim

I first met Carmelo Anthony when he was nineteen years old, fresh off an NCAA championship in his one year at Syracuse. The most talented college player in years was coming to me to help him prepare for the draft, and I couldn't wait to oblige.

He had learned about me from Juan Dixon, his friend from Baltimore; they spoke often back then, and once Melo declared for the NBA draft, Juan invited him to train with us. While they laced their shoes, I quickly modified the workout I'd planned to an intense but shortened session, pairing shooting and ball-handling with quickness, agility, speed, and conditioning.

Sixty minutes passed quickly. Afterward, Melo sat on the gym floor, his back against the wall, wrists on his bent knees, relieved he had survived our first session. I sat on the floor beside him.

I wondered whether he truly understood how immensely talented he was. A blind man could recognize that a player like Melo came around once in a generation. He had a remarkable combination of size, strength, agility, skill, tenacity, and fearlessness. He even had "it," a marketer's dream, something I could see from the moment he strutted into the gym. He was charming, photogenic, and possessed a soulful first name that matched his aura. He was going to make an NBA team really happy and his agent really wealthy. I hoped they'd both understand how to connect with him and blend his physical gifts with his dynamic and textured personality. That was my goal as well.

Whatever flaws I saw in his offensive efficiency, shot mechanics, weight, conditioning, and quickness could be addressed with short workouts like the one we just had. Tutoring happens in sixty-minute sessions, but training the mind, body, and soul to make dramatic and lasting adaptations requires real time. I hoped he would become amazing in every aspect of his performance, outlook, and behavior, from the instant he wakes up to the moment he kisses his son good night.

I had known Melo for only a few minutes, but everything about him whispered, *Cool*. He walked at what seemed like a deliberate cool pace, took his time putting on his shoes, took his time warming up, took his time chatting with Juan before beginning the workout. He never rushed. I wondered if this pace was somehow reflected in his game as well—that to date he had purposely played at the speed limit as a built-in alibi in case he fell short of his goals, like an exceptionally bright student who rationalizes average grades by claiming the subject matter bores him. How great could he be if he opened the throttle as far as it would go? Consistent effort, intensity, and a hypersonic pace would batter his opponents and set him on the road to becoming one of the best ever to play the game, and I was already certain he was capable of it.

He was a Ferrari and I wanted him to take his engine for a

spin on the Autobahn. I am guilty of sometimes imposing my wants and wishes on others, so at that moment I wondered whether I wanted this for him more than he wanted it for himself. I was determined to help bring about this change, and if I wasn't welcome, Melo could politely tell me to leave him the fuck alone.

I knew I couldn't just walk into his life as if it were the lobby of the Marriott. Superstars protect themselves with layers of people and feelings of distrust. I had to first build rapport with him, and I started by telling him I remembered seeing him play "PB"—pre-braids. He laughed, and I described to him the Melo I watched one afternoon at the Adidas ABCD Camp in New Jersey: a supremely confident fifteen-year-old, playing with his shoes untied, who wore his hair in an afro along with a headband stenciled with the letters *HOBO*—Helping Our Brothers Out, a store in DC. I mentioned our mutual acquaintance Kevin Braswell, a former guard at Georgetown University, who first told me about a teenager from Baltimore who, after a massive growth spurt, carried himself with remarkable swag and was destined for NBA stardom.

"He predicted the future," I said as Melo nodded.

That instant, I felt like we'd connected, that I'd made it through the first few layers of insulation. We shook hands before I left the gym. We didn't discuss scheduling future workouts—something I would have loved, but I didn't want to suggest it at the time. If I'd chased him, the relationship would have been doomed from the start, because people want what they cannot have. I hoped he would take the initiative with me, because it would minimize feelings of entitlement and he'd be more likely to train with an open mind. I didn't know when I would see him again, but had faith I eventually would.

And so it began with a call from Melo several days later. One session became a few sessions, which became several weeks and months and years. The relationship grew over time, in stages, and became layered: trainer to confidant to friend, to the point years later where I consider him like family. Despite our obvious differences, we understand each other's temperament, style, and rhythm.

I was unassuming while he could intimidate. I could be neurotic while he was cool as a Popsicle. I was goofy while he was smooth. I was defiant while he preferred to not ruffle feathers, unless pushed into a corner. I remained in the shadows while he was the source of the spotlight. I grinned while he laughed. I was content with simplicity while he savored the details in luxury. I was punctual while he was "on his way." I wasn't a good employee while he was a great teammate. I analyzed while he accepted things for what they were. I worried while he assumed things would be fine. I saved for a rainy day while he was generous. I expected one more while he considered less as more.

We respected each other's differences. I learned to see him for what he was and could be, rather than what others thought he wasn't. Much of what he "wasn't" was tied to an uninformed public perception of an incredibly gifted player who didn't open all of his gifts and was easily lured into poor decisions. That was not the Melo I knew. And even if Melo acted in ways that didn't jibe with my sensibilities, I never micromanaged, judged, or scolded him. I could not expect our sensibilities to mirror each other. We grew up in different communities and we had different priorities. Youth, fame, and fortune meant that anything he wanted was just a fingertip away.

I also never preached to him, even when he ran late, which was often. I don't necessarily see the correlation between punctuality and professionalism that's so important to everyone else. I recognize he might feel that making others wait tilts the perception of importance in his favor. I don't have to agree in order to understand and accept it.

That doesn't mean I don't push him. I always prod Melo. I always remind him I think he could be the greatest. I tell him he could be the best in the world. "Doesn't it bother you they don't talk about you the way they do about Bron and KD?" I always nudge him to be even greater than he is.

When I think about Melo the person, I think about a session we had in the summer of 2007 at the Verizon Center in Washington, DC. He came thirty minutes late, and to my surprise, he arrived pushing his young son in his baby stroller. He explained he'd given his then-fiancée, La La Vazquez, a spa day for her birthday and promised he would watch the boy.

He gripped the stroller handles tightly and slowly let momentum carry him and the stroller down the ramp that ran parallel with the court. The ramp has a relatively high grade to make life easier for the arena maintenance and equipment managers carrying heavy equipment into the gym. He parked the stroller far enough from the court to eliminate any chance of it being struck by a ball, yet close enough so he could hear his son. He lifted the sunshade on the stroller and gently touched the baby's face.

As arguably the most gifted offensive player in the NBA, Melo prefers to focus on what he does best: shoot and score. But I insist he also work on areas we agree need improvement: defense, footwork, quickness, ball-handling, work rate, and intensity. He can put on weight, so he has to be careful about his diet. Any weight gain would limit his mobility, so we always emphasize conditioning while he trains. I know how hectic his off-season calendar can be, so I let him direct the intensity of the workouts on those days when he lets me know he just doesn't have it.

In general, I keep workouts focused and tight with minimal interruption for things like water or conversation because the theme of efficiency is paramount. Also, I don't want the player to think he's running things, as if he is bigger than the game. With younger players or players I haven't worked with often, during the session they may interrupt a drill by asking me a question, and all the while I'm thinking, *You're just talking to me because you want to rest. Talk to me later.* But over the years, you learn whom you can trust, who stops for a reason. If we have a relationship and things have become more advanced, and a player wants to stop, ask questions, grab water—then, sure, of course. And obviously Melo and I have been in that place for a while.

So it was now mid-June, and he hadn't run hard since the season ended. We started with some light shooting, then ramped up the intensity to include shooting drills paired with full-court sprints. After just a short time, he stopped and ran over to the sideline.

It's only been ten minutes. There is no way he could be tired already, I thought.

Only then did I hear the baby crying. The sounds of the ball hitting the rim and bouncing from the floor had muffled his cries. Melo pulled a small towel from the diaper bag that rested below the belly of the stroller. He lifted the boy and rested the baby's head on the towel on his shoulder. His son continued to cry, so Melo tapped him lightly on the back to comfort him. Melo's huge tattoo-covered hands swallowed the boy as he carried him in his arms around the court, whispering in his ear and gently massaging his back. The cries subsided.

We went back to our drills. Within thirty minutes, I heard another cry.

"Hold on for a sec," Melo said as he again jogged to the stroller. When he got there, he laughed and said to his boy, "Why you fakin'? You cryin' and you don't even have any tears." He pushed the stroller around the perimeter of the court.

The crying again subsided once they crossed half-court. Melo whispered to him. He parked the stroller near the equipment room. Then his phone rang.

"Yooooo, what up? Everything's under control. He's sleepin' now. (Pause) How you like the spa?"

I assumed La La had called. I jogged to the corner to retrieve the basketball, but mostly just to give him some privacy. I heard him laugh loudly. He was obviously in good spirits.

I thought, *It's a shame people make so many assumptions about him.* They see a tatted-up kid who's made a few poor choices, gotten into some trouble, been in some fights, who's considered a street kid—but that doesn't mean they know him or know anything about him. This is the same kid who's so incredibly generous to so many people and doesn't advertise his good deeds. As for the tattoos, they are simply his form of expression— the same way he loves Muhammad Ali photographs and artwork, or has art commissioned for his home, or has an interest in fashion. But the world chooses to see a diva or a thug.

It doesn't help that he's had a few well-publicized incidents on the court. I was there on the night in December 2006 at Madison Square Garden when Melo came to the defense of his teammate JR Smith after the Knicks' Mardy Collins had pulled Smith down by the neck on a breakaway. It was a hard and ugly foul in a game that Melo's Nuggets had in hand, leading by nineteen with just over a minute to go. Collins and Denver's Smith got up and continued to argue. Referees and teammates tried to separate the players. Melo entered the melee to aid his teammates, words were exchanged, and Melo punched Mardy Collins in the face and then backpedaled to the other end of the court, chased by Jared Jeffries and Nate Robinson of the Knicks.

All ten players on the court were ejected, but Melo drew the most criticism. It was two years after the melee between the Pistons and Pacers in Auburn Hills, and the NBA was hypersensitive to incidents of player violence. A lot of people thought a star of Melo's caliber should know better than to throw a punch and risk a suspension.

I always tell my guys, if you want to make franchise money, be prepared to take franchise heat. I waited for Melo in the bowels of Madison Square Garden that night, and he was his usual calm, cool self, smiling, telling friends and family, "I'm aight. I'm cool."

He was ultimately suspended for fifteen games, which cost him more than $600,000 in salary. He had the right to appeal, but he announced that he was going to accept the punishment rather than dragging things out and focusing more attention on the fight. He also apologized to the league, to his team, and to Collins.

There's no question it hurt his image, but I wonder if the people who judged him have any idea what it would be like to be in his shoes at the moment. How many competing thoughts were running through his mind at once? *Do I step in? Do I defend my teammate? Do I risk a suspension and huge fine when I have a responsibility to family and friends who look to me for support? Do I look like a sucker if I don't fight?*

Players are taught to be tough and to have their teammates' backs. The game is played with intensity. It's also played by many men who grew up in communities where toughness commands a particularly high level of respect. Some people saw Melo rescuing a teammate, knowing full well that there would be a cost to him personally. By doing so, he maintained respect in the neighborhood, something we cannot minimize if we didn't grow up with that frame of reference. Street credibility is the equivalent of an Ivy League résumé in some communities.

So what if some people saw him as a punk for getting in a fight? Other people would have thought the same thing if he hadn't. And he knew that the people who mattered were the ones who actually know him, who don't make up their minds about him based on his actions in an instant.

Same thing in his well-publicized beef with Kevin Garnett in 2013. There are lines you don't cross when you're talking shit on the court. KG crossed them, Melo reined himself in on the court, then went looking for him after the game. He showed the control in-game that people wanted from him in the earlier scuffle but couldn't let KG's words go by without a challenge. Damned if you do, damned if you don't, damned if you do or don't at the right or wrong time.

And none of that stuff—in two moments six years apart— means a fraction as much as the gentle, loving, generous guy I know, taking a moment from his workout to comfort his infant son so his fiancée can catch a break for a day.

Diva? Thug? More like a great basketball player and teammate, and an even better father, husband, son, and friend.

More than ten years have passed since Melo and I first shared the court together. Since that time, I have seen him shine with the ball in his hands, recognize he can't make everyone happy, reinvent himself on and off the court, embrace his interests and differences, tattoo professional basketball with his legacy, celebrate the birth of a lovely son and a marriage to a wonderful woman, grieve the tragic and unimaginable loss of a sibling, and learn to handle success and disappointment with grace.

Melo soared to a new level during the 2012–2013 season. Had it not been for injuries to his ankle, knee, and shoulder, I'm fairly certain he could have averaged more than thirty points per game and taken his team even further into the playoffs. Even with the injuries, he earned his first NBA scoring title. I heard ad nauseam the critics who harped on his volume of shots, low percentages, and statistical inefficiency. Yes to all the above. But while statistics may help draw conclusions, they don't often show rationale and context. Melo's genius lies in what I call his faith. His faith in himself enables him to fail and succeed without regret, to expect an even better next game, to consider his bad shot a better option than his teammates' good shot, to believe his defender will never have a chance, and to believe he has a responsibility to shoulder the burden of his team.

And for the skeptics, I also want to give context to what it means to average nearly twenty-nine points per game. For most players in the NBA, twenty-nine points in a game would be a success, twenty-nine points a week would win Player of the Week honors, and twenty-nine points a month would make you Player of the Month in a runaway. Now imagine averaging twenty-nine points over the course of six months against sophisticated defenses and even better defenders whose sole purpose is to stop you.

I texted Melo when he won the scoring title: "I am very proud of you. Few people on this planet could appreciate what it meant and what it took to achieve this. Keep shining."

"Yessssir," he replied. "We (me and u) did it."

I didn't answer. It was one of those occasions when a reply would have tarnished the moment and its message. He knew me well enough to know what it meant to me. I saved the message and showed it to my mom. I even read it from time to time when I would become impatient with my progress and with my journey. It would quickly center me and put me back on course in the direction of happiness. It reminded me of my purpose and why our lives had intersected.

Mark Twain said it best: "I can live for two months on a good compliment."

CHAPTER THIRTEEN

STACK

gifts w/o a return address = real acts of kindness
#anonymous #precious

In June 2004, I watched Jerry Stackhouse, who at the time played for the Washington Wizards, casually shoot his jump shot while I sat along the sidelines of his team's practice facility. I was waiting for Juan Dixon, who was also with the Wizards, to shower and change after our earlier workout.

"Drop the ball," I called out, raising my voice so he could hear me over the sound of the ball hitting the floor.

"Huh?"

He was practicing his reverse pivot, starting with his back to the basket, then swinging his leg, torso, and the ball around before he shot. I noticed he held the ball at waist level when he made the move.

I rose from my seat to pull all 6-6, 215 pounds of him by his sleeve so I could turn his back to me. "This is where their hands will probably sit," I said as I motioned for him to look at my hands, stationed at his midsection. "You can exploit your defender this way. Make sure your ball placement avoids their hands when you pivot."

When an offensive player has his back to the defender, that defender will generally have his hands roughly waist high. As the offensive player turns, he can avoid the defender's hands by bringing the ball up and over their hands or swinging it low.

Without hesitation Jerry turned to face me as I passed him the ball, then shifted again so his back was to the basket. He internally rotated his left foot until it and his shoulders were square with the rim. He swung the ball below his knee from left to right, and took one dribble forward with his right hand for a short jump shot near the left elbow. He moved deliberately to mimic the proper ball placement and footwork we had just discussed. Each time the ball fell through the net, it added a tablespoon of confidence and trust in the stranger he had just met. I glanced at my phone twenty minutes later.

"Looks good so far, Stack," I said as I headed to the sidelines to grab my gym bag. "I gotta run. By the way, my name is Idan."

"Good to meet you, man," he said. Then he snatched my arm. "Yo-o-o-o, who else do you work with?"

I listed a few players.

"What's your number so we can connect?" he asked.

I gave him my cell. "Hit me, we'll figure out something."

I can't say how many times I'd watched Jerry suspend himself in midair while he played for the University of North Carolina, the Philadelphia 76ers, the Detroit Pistons, and now the Washington Wizards. Ten years and one thousand games later, his body had been battered by the jabs and uppercuts that only time and professional basketball can deliver. For professional athletes, deteriorating superpowers force them to make adjustments to prolong their careers. For Jerry, that meant relying more on skill, efficiency, strategy, and conditioning than on athleticism. I hoped I would hear from him, but I wasn't "thirsty," as the athletes would say.

He called.

On our first day together, I suggested he dribble with his legs bent, not his back, and his eyes focused on the rim and not the floor. The transition from playing ball in the air to playing it on the ground wouldn't happen overnight. If he could master the ball, he would feel liberated, like the way we feel when we first earn our driver's license. He struggled, but that was important; struggle leads to humility, and humility leads to learning.

Afterward Jerry asked when we would reconnect. That was like hearing my favorite song.

Soon I was traveling with him so we wouldn't miss training days because of his busy off-season calendar. I enjoyed Jerry's company on the road because we shared things in common, besides our love for ball and our quest to improve his game. We were both raised in religious homes; his mother was a minister and mine taught Old Testament classes. We talked about religion, its importance, its place, and its complexity. While I've distanced myself from organized religion, I still want to know if it fits somewhere in my life. Jerry was devout and tithed regularly to the church. I asked him once whether he wanted control over the money he donates. He considered it like sewing strings into those dollar bills, which would detract from the act of selfless giving. He was content to hope they would do right with the money. I told him that in Judaism, anonymous gifts were considered the most precious. He liked that.

Jerry wanted me to travel with him and his family to North Carolina over the extended Fourth of July weekend. Spending five days trapped in North Carolina humidity didn't sound appetizing, but then I remembered that a year ago I was sitting behind a desk drafting memos at a law firm and dreaming about chances like this, so of course I said yes.

We flew to Raleigh and then drove to Chapel Hill. It was

my first time in Tar Heel country. Wherever we went, the community treated him like basketball royalty; he would always be a representative of the University of North Carolina to them, no matter how many NBA teams he played for. They stared at him with admiration and welcomed him home.

The next day my cell phone rang in the early morning. "You ready?" he asked.

"Ready for what?"

"We leavin' in ten minutes. Meet me in the lobby."

I'd assumed we'd spend the weekend training in Chapel Hill. Jerry had never mentioned any other cities. *Shame on me for not asking him*, I thought. Jerry could change his mind faster than Sarah Jessica Parker changes shoes. He was temperamental and demanding, but I never took it personally and got used to following his lead. That's just the way it is with some of the high-profile guys; they're used to being CEOs of their world, and you have to adapt to their clock. I didn't negotiate on these issues, and I didn't micromanage; he was my guy and absorbing such inconveniences and eccentricities was part of the package.

On our way to Jerry's hometown of Kinston, North Carolina, we stopped at a local diner. A busboy approached our table to wipe it clean. Jerry glanced over at him, and soon he was staring.

"Holy sheaaaat," Jerry exclaimed, which startled the man.

The man stood upright and tucked the rag into the front pocket of his apron.

"Oh my goodness," he answered.

"Good Laaawd. How the hell you been?" Jerry asked.

He wiped his hands on the apron and exchanged man hugs with Jerry. He reluctantly waved as he forced a smile toward me and Jerry's family. Ever since I was young, I could create whole storyboards to go along with the things I sensed in a moment around me. I saw the flash of melancholy from Jerry's friend, and I instantly envisioned that they last saw each other as teenagers before Jerry left their small town to catch his dreams, while his friend, for whatever reason, never left. Seeing Jerry immediately reminded him that you can't press rewind on life.

After a few small bites, Jerry gently pushed his plate forward and rested his napkin on the plate. He watched his young children nibble. He glanced over again at his friend, who was busy bussing plates from the other tables. He rubbed his bald head a few more times. He motioned for the bill. I saw him peel several hundred-dollar bills and some singles from a thin wad of cash he carried. He rested the money on his lap and began to meticulously fold each of the hundred-dollar bills until they resembled skinny cigarettes. He fanned the single bills on the table as if he were dealing a hand of poker. He then slid the hundreds beneath the singles. He signaled for his friend. They hugged and shook hands.

We walked toward the car, but I could still see the man through the restaurant windows. He cleared the table, then suddenly realized what his old friend had left him.

It was a thoughtful gesture, performed with grace, humility, and respect for a man's pride. Unlike the celebrities whose publicists issue press releases whenever their client makes a contribution, Jerry did everything he could to avoid calling attention to it. If I hadn't been sitting where I could see what he did, I would have never known.

His gift was the purest kind.

CHAPTER FOURTEEN

A CRY FOR HELP

thank God 4 tears, without them they wouldn't
appreciate how much we care
#tearFULL

I t was late in the evening at the Verizon Center in Washington, DC, and I'd just finished a session with Jerry Stackhouse in the practice facility when the doors swung open with great force. A young woman in a Washington Mystics uniform sprinted down the stairs and past me cupping a WNBA ball as if she were going for a first down. She positioned herself a few feet from the basket, squared her shoulders, and sent the ball out of her hands as fast as she could. She missed shot after shot and sprinted after the ball each time before tossing it again at the rim without aiming. It looked like an on-court version of the arcade game where players shoot small rubber basketballs into a hoop as fast as they can for sixty seconds.

The woman shooting the ball was Alana Beard, who had been the second pick in the WNBA draft several weeks earlier.

She was a star at Duke, a three-time All-American, and a Wooden Award winner as the national Player of the Year in her senior season. And here she was, having come directly from a game, no shower, no change of clothes, flinging up shots with tears streaming down her cheeks. I felt her sadness immediately.

"It's OK," I said, heading onto the court without waiting for an introduction.

"It's OK what?" Alana answered as she chased down her missed shots. The remnants of salt from her earlier tears had left white streaks across her caramel-colored cheeks.

"To feel frustrated," I replied.

She let the ball roll into the corner after it hit the rim.

"I can't believe how shitty I just played. I can't make a shot. I can't do anything right." She struggled to complete her thoughts as her frustration played havoc with her words.

Before the tears could make a reappearance, she dashed to retrieve the ball. She again wiped her eyes with her wrist. I sensed her embarrassment that a stranger had seen her so vulnerable. The gym was supposed to be empty. I gently grabbed her by the wrist and led her toward the corner, near the three-point line.

"Let's work on a few things I do with my NBA guys," I said.

I'm sure she had no idea who I was or why I was even at the facility. There wasn't any reason she should know, and I wasn't concerned about it one way or another. I saw an athlete in distress—a star in her world, but just another struggling player on the practice floor in front of me—and I felt a responsibility to help out.

Over the years other players had cried in front of me. Tears were like the bread crumbs in the Hansel and Gretel fable: They led me to the source of vulnerability. I wasn't a therapist, a psychologist, a social worker, or even a counselor, but I could empathize and understand a player's frustration when the thing we love the most doesn't yield the results we had hoped for. Some say never offer advice unless asked. I say people are often crying inside, so I don't only look for their tears as a cue.

I didn't know Alana, but I thought I could help her improve and ease her frustrations by getting her away from trying to overcome her struggles by doing the same thing but harder.

I suspected that the WNBA, like the NBA, was filled with long, athletic, and skilled players who can rotate faster and recover better on defense than the players she'd faced in college. And I figured that Alana, like the NBA players I worked with, would have to recognize situations quicker and become more efficient.

We spent the next hour working on situations where I thought Alana would catch the ball in scoring positions. I had her pass me the ball at the low post and then move to the wing laterally in a defensive slide for her shot. I recommended she begin that slide as soon as her defender turned her head to offer help defense on the low post. The defensive slide would keep her shoulders square with the rim, which would expedite the release of her shot. Running to the wing, as she was used to doing, meant she would have to rotate her hips to square her shoulders to the rim before shooting, and this extra movement gave the defender enough time to recover and challenge her shot.

Over the course of the hour, she grew engaged and accepted the drills without questioning their purpose. The tears subsided and she seemed calmer, probably thanks to a combination of fatigue and the realization that it took only a few minutes to remedy some of the problem. The ball fell repeatedly through the net as she moved with game speed across gamelike scenarios, getting her shot off quicker without rushing her release.

Moving and shooting and trying something new brought the joy of play back into the game for Alana that night. She had been making something simple so hard. Basketball is a game we fall in love with as kids, and I always try to reach the child inside every player because kids have the ability to find joy and simplicity in whatever they do. I don't know if it mattered what I suggested to her; she's a great player, and she'd have figured it out eventually on her own. It was probably as important that I talked with her calmly, with empathy and understanding; often it's not what you say as much as how you say it.

Alana asked if we could meet again. I didn't consult with her agent or her team; we just agreed to a schedule of workouts for the next few days. We didn't talk about expectations or the areas of her game we'd work on, or even training fees—not yet. We just exchanged numbers.

Alana and I got together in the early morning until she left for an extended West Coast road trip with her team. They were the first of our many sessions over the next several years, as she developed into a four-time WNBA All-Star, a standout on both ends of the court. If I remember right, she averaged more than twenty points per game during those away games after we began to work together. I suspected the short bout with success reminded her of what she was capable of. Several days later I read that Alana had given me credit for the difference in her play.

She made the effort, I thought. *She played the game and she deserves all the glory.* I often felt uncomfortable accepting thanks or praise or gifts from athletes I worked with. My mom sometimes reminds me that accepting gifts shouldn't be such a challenge because I embrace the gifts the heavens had handed me: a love for the game, empathy, intuition, compassion, and faith.

My mom is right.

CHAPTER FIFTEEN

THE LEGEND OF KEVIN DURANT

success and humility can coexist
#KD

To hear the basketball world tell it, you'd think the heavens had conspired with the parents of Kevin Durant to create the perfect modern superstar and role model. It's not enough that he's nearly seven feet tall with limbs as long as tree branches; he also moves with the deft precision of a luxury sports car, shoots the ball with the accuracy of an army sniper, has a devotion to his craft that borders on religious, is as humble as a Tibetan monk and generous as a cross between Santa Claus and the Tooth Fairy.

Too good to be true? Yes. But it's all true anyway.

I'd heard him described as one of a kind, but people in the league say that about a lot of guys who turn out to be products of hope rather than divine inspiration. I had to see for myself, so I invited Kevin to a pre-draft workout in June 2009 with Stephen

Curry, Wes Matthews, and Sam Young, all three of whom made the league and are still in it. Kevin had just finished his second NBA season and was the youngest of the four.

"Workouts start at seven on Saturday morning. Come alone," I said.

I arrived fifteen minutes early to make sure someone had unlocked the doors leading to the gym. I saw a parked car in the lot, and I figured it belonged to a custodian. When I got closer, I recognized Kevin's profile. He had the seat reclined and was listening to music. I gently tapped on the passenger window to not alarm him.

"You never get a second chance to make a first impression," he later told a *Sports Illustrated* reporter about our first session.

Stephen, Wes, and Sam arrived after seven. Everyone greeted each other as if they already knew one another—a consequence of fame and the collective brotherhood of elite basketball players. We made small talk as we laced up our shoes. I didn't let on that I still felt surprised a budding NBA star would carve time out of his weekend morning just weeks after his season ended to train alongside players who were junior in experience and ability. We began with just a short warm-up, which I prefer because players don't get to spend ten minutes shooting on the sideline before they check in to a game. We quickly progressed to multiple sets of full-court sprints that finished with jump shots from both corners and wings and the top of the key. As they fatigued, I intensified the drill: Now they would finish their full-court sprints with one- and two-dribble jump shots from the same spots on the court.

Early in Kevin's professional career, some critics thought he'd have trouble with the physical play in the NBA because he couldn't bench-press 185 pounds at the NBA Pre-Draft Camp. This proved about as accurate as forecasting a snowstorm for Honolulu. That morning I witnessed him release the ball effortlessly from what seemed like a nearby football field; control the ball with his massive hands yet with the dexterity of a potter; sprint the length of the court without his heels touching the ground; maneuver his feet during two-ball dribbling drills with the agility of a defensive back; and quickly master any drill I threw his way. The game came so easy to him that I worried Stephen, Wes, and Sam might feel discouraged, because Kevin's obvious gifts could exaggerate the distance between them and the NBA's elite. But then I heard him praise the three of them, which left me wondering if he could read minds too.

Kevin possessed extraordinary physical gifts and a deep reverence for the game. He was also modest, and hadn't yet made an All-Star team, but one morning in a gym showed me that he had scoring titles and all-NBA recognition in his future—and a shot at being one of the greatest ever.

Two years later, I found myself sitting on the floor of a gym in LA with Kevin, Los Angeles Clippers star Blake Griffin, and JR Smith, then with the Denver Nuggets. The three guys were exhausted from ninety minutes of intense effort. Only hours earlier, Kevin was home in Washington, DC, reading a message I'd sent from my BlackBerry: "I'm in LA with Blake. Let's get some work in."

He'd grabbed a backpack, flown cross-country on a moment's notice, and now here we were.

The session included sprinting to different spots on the court, catching the ball at different angles, rotating their feet and shoulders in different directions, and finishing near the basket with different shot selections. I don't waste time having guys just stand and shoot; they don't play ball standing still, so we don't train that way either. I capped off their session with games of one-on-one, played with their backs to the basket, from the low block, wing and elbow, and with dribble and time parameters.

I took many factors into consideration before putting Kevin, Blake, and JR together as workout partners, like I do with any such group. Talent, personality, station in life, size, goals, commitment, strengths, weaknesses, friendship, circle of friends—it all weighs in. For instance, Chris Paul can work with Melo or LeBron because they're close friends, partly because they share a rarefied status in the world of pop culture; there are very few people who live the kind of life they do. On that level, it's like Brad Pitt marrying Angelina Jolie, or Jay Z and Beyoncé—the superfamous stay among their own. Of course, Chris and Melo and LeBron also have enormous respect and admiration for one another, and are motivated to become not merely great but the greatest ever to play.

Blake has the body of a superhero, and I wanted Kevin to have to work against Blake's herculean strength. The best way for him to confront any possible self-doubt about his lack of muscle would be to socialize Kevin to contact, especially with his back to the basket. I hoped Blake would pound Kevin mercilessly, and that Kevin would combat it with finesse and technique and by retaliating with his own aggressive play. For instance, Kevin would have to adjust the position where he holds the ball while he rotates to attack the basket in order to avoid Blake's quick swipe with his hands. Meanwhile, Blake recognizes that he fades back on his own shot and relies on power around the basket to compensate for a low release point. He's 6-10 with long arms, but sometimes his hands are down near his face when he shoots, which makes him a lot smaller. I wanted him to lengthen everything and utilize all of his athleticism and his length. It's okay to fade back, but if you fade back small—shooting with your hands too low—you've minimized the physical gifts that make you special. Kevin's own wingspan is insane, so no matter how much Blake fades back, he can't fade back enough that Kevin can't touch the ball unless Blake extends his arms. I wanted Kevin's length to force Blake to consciously lift the release on his shot and his jump hook.

As for JR, I genuinely believe he can be an elite player, and I wanted him to see the effort of the league's best players and to start approaching the game with similar dedication. In exchange for his commitment to treat basketball with the same reverence as the NBA's finest, I had promised I would pair him with them, hoping they would all come to view one another as peers and overturn the perception that JR was just another great talent who underachieved.

It's possible to change a player's behavior and patterns of movement over time through careful, repeated instruction—but it can happen faster by putting him in an environment that magnifies his weaknesses and forces him to adapt. These are smart, off-the-charts competitive guys, and when they have to, they'll find a way to become comfortable with the uncomfortable.

For the remainder of the morning Kevin absorbed contact and used his backside and shoulders to take position away from Blake; Blake attempted to raise his release point above Kevin's outstretched hands; and with every basket made, JR became infused with more faith that he belonged with the NBA's best. They played one-on-one, fouled hard, attacked each other's weakness, fought to win, and yet also clapped their hands, shouted encouragement, reminded one another of proper mechanics, spotted inconsistencies in effort, helped each other off the ground and wiped dry the sweat that pooled on the wood floor. These were the moments I wished I could share with the world: On the most ordinary of days in an empty, nondescript gym a few minutes after sunrise, challenging the world's best basketball players to compete like gladiators at the highest level under strenuous circumstances specifically designed to fatigue, test, and build, and witnessing the camaraderie and respect they had for one another.

I watched in amazement.

I had encouraged them to battle wholeheartedly, and they

responded by showing me it was possible to fight fair. In their hands, a competitive game became a kind of spiritual transcendence and an expression of love.

It was pure, it was thrilling, and it was legendary. It may have been too good, but it was definitely true.

CHAPTER SIXTEEN

ZERO

how bad must they b in order 4 u
to forget all their good
#scale

They called him dangerous, thoughtless, manipulative, stupid, and unappreciative. Hearing all the negative talk made me uncomfortable, because none of it sounded like the person I'd come to know over the years in the gym. I made my own inquiries, read whatever I could find, but I still couldn't make sense of how a basketball-obsessed, benevolent overachiever could become an object of almost complete public scorn.

When I think about Gilbert Arenas, the joy he takes in the game, and his overall quest for fun and thrills, I'm reminded of how it felt to run down a steep grass-covered hill in my childhood, going as fast as I could until I eventually tumbled.

Gilbert wasn't supposed to be an NBA star. He wore number o at the University of Arizona because that's how many minutes some people predicted he'd play his first year. Somehow he finished second on that team in scoring, then led the Wildcats to the NCAA Finals the next year before declaring for the draft.

Gilbert was chosen with the thirty-first pick, the second selection in the second round. Eighteen teams passed on him. The number 0 again was a motivating factor, reminding him of people's expectations. He rocketed to NBA All-Star status, but became even better known for his fall. Toward the end of the 2007 season he tore the medial collateral ligament in his knee against the Charlotte Bobcats. He barely played during the next two years while struggling to fully recover from his injury; in the middle of that period the Wizards signed him to a six-year, $111 million contract, which brought a lot of attention to a different set of zeroes. And just when he was finally finding himself on the court again—a triple double in mid-December 2009, followed six days later by a forty-five-point night—a practical joke between teammates went terribly wrong, and the NBA suspended Gilbert for the rest of the season after he pleaded guilty to a felony gun charge. Things have never been the same.

During the spring of 2010 I invited Gilbert to train alongside Eric Bledsoe while I prepared Eric for the NBA draft. I hoped time on the court would briefly calm the turbulence in Gilbert's life. Eric was excited to work with an NBA All-Star he'd always admired, and he trained hard that morning to try to win Gilbert's approval.

Afterward, Gil and I sat along the sidelines and talked as we always did at the end of our workouts. He talked about the aftermath of the incident in furious detail. I didn't ask him for the details of what happened, but as I understand it from conversations with other people and an excellent article by Daniel Wattenberg at Reason.com, this is the story: Gilbert and his teammate Javaris Crittenton were playing cards, and there was a dispute between the two of them. They bantered back and forth, and at one point Javaris said they'd have to fight over it; Gilbert joked that he was too old for a fight, but not too old to shoot

Javaris in the face. Javaris said he would bring his own gun and shoot Gilbert in the knee he'd just spent so much time rehabbing.

At the next practice, Gilbert brought four unloaded guns into the locker room and put them on a chair by Javaris's locker along with a sign that said PICK ONE. It was a joke—a misguided joke. Javaris picked up one of the guns and threw it along the floor at Gilbert, then pulled his own gun out of his backpack just to show Gilbert he had one. That was it; that was the whole incident, and the guys were joking about it together in a matter of minutes.

Somehow, a week or two later a tabloid reporter heard about the guns and wrote it up as if it were the Gunfight at the O.K. Corral. It wasn't anything of the kind. Gilbert's guns weren't loaded, and neither of the men ever pointed a gun at the other. The story exploded across the airwaves and the Internet, and nobody wanted to hear about what actually happened. Gilbert and his teammates tried to make light of it during pregame introductions one time—after all, they knew it wasn't something serious and dangerous—but that only made things worse. The next thing Gilbert knew, he was suspended indefinitely and pleading guilty to a felony charge.

I understand that NBA commissioner David Stern was in a tough position, needing to take a strong stand against guns and always mindful of the damage such an incident could do to the league's image. They say a lie can travel halfway around the world while the truth is putting on its shoes; the public perception of this nonevent was created by the inaccurate tabloid report, and any denials coming from the witnesses or participants were dismissed as a cover-up. Even the head of the players union made comments in response to the imagined scene rather than waiting for the facts.

Sitting there with Gilbert, I could see his justifiable anger that he'd been betrayed by the league, his team, and his community.

How could one dumb act negate thousands of good deeds? In a flash, everyone forgot all about his generosity, about the thousands of good things he's done for people, about his Zero Two Hero Foundation and its donations to schools, kids, shelters, victims of natural disasters, the homeless, and on and on. They were so quick to condemn him and lump him with other serial offenders—a misjudgment that Wattenberg's article described as "like comparing Inspector Clouseau to Inspector 'Dirty Harry' Callahan."

It was cathartic for him to vent to an audience he trusted, so I listened; most people had stopped listening to him by now. That was one of the harshest consequences of pleading guilty to a crime he didn't consider criminal or malicious—even worse than a month of incarceration in a halfway house for prisoners on the verge of parole. You can debate facts, fairness, and justice all day long, and I believe he had all these things on his side of the argument, but doing so would eventually kill his spirit, destroy the self-described "goofball" I had come to know so well.

The Gilbert I remember found inspiration from his critics, a group that multiplied after his suspension. His knee still needed to get stronger, and now so did his spirit and reputation; I hoped he would turn the criticism into motivation and strive in earnest to return to the NBA. As he said in his commercial for Adidas in happier times, "If nobody believes in you, anything you do is a positive. . . . The reason I wear number zero is because it lets me know I need to go out there and fight every day."

The Gilbert I remember obsessed about the game, preferring empty practice gyms, odd hours, and sleeping on the couch in the players' lounge at the arena when he was too tired to drive home after a late night of training. And he rarely advertised his effort, unlike some players who use social media as a microphone to magnify their work ethic.

The Gilbert I remember had charm and a sense of humor, although his timing needed work. He could launch into a politically incorrect joke in front of any group of people and laugh about it the whole time.

The Gilbert I remember was Santa Claus year-round to children. He greeted everyone with such sincerity and made them feel like they were the only one in the room. His good deeds were legendary, like the time he encouraged an equipment manager to lose weight and rewarded him with thousands of dollars, or when he befriended a young boy who lost his family to a house fire.

Gilbert continued to rehab his knee, and even gave the NBA another chance. There was something missing, however; he didn't play with the same recklessness and confidence. I wondered whether he had fully recovered from the injury. I wondered too whether he felt like a divorcee among happily married couples when he joined his new team. The incident, suspension, and trial created issues of trust for him, and he couldn't help wondering if he could trust the people around him, or even his own judgment anymore.

He's still chasing the ball, most recently in China, playing for the team Yao Ming owns, the Shanghai Sharks. The Chinese season is just thirty-two games, but even there he missed about half of them with a groin injury. Most Chinese teams expect their American players to be the top scorers, and Gilbert was happy to have the green light again, a very different situation from his later NBA experiences riding the bench.

I worry about him. Did he become addicted to the sensational highs of his epic pre-injury performances? Is his self-esteem so intertwined with his game that, without basketball and the applause, he'll feel empty? Is he tormented by the fear he can no longer live up to what people remember of him, like a homecoming queen afraid to attend her high school reunion? He wore people's low expectations of him like a badge of honor for so long; what does he do when his body won't let him meet expectations he's worked hard to raise?

Time has its way with everyone. Eventually it will call on him to walk away from the game. Leaving on his terms with one last toss of his jersey into the stands would be the curtain call he deserves. I wondered whether all this could have been avoided if he had walked down the steep grass-covered hill, if he could have avoided the tumble. But that wasn't the Gil I knew. Running as fast as he can was what he did best.

CHAPTER SEVENTEEN

THE EMPEROR

it ain't a basket until the ball falls through the net
#dontcounthemchickens2early

Late one evening in 2010 I missed a call from a restricted number, then immediately received a text message from an unfamiliar area code. I recognized the name at the end of the message. Anyone with the slightest awareness of basketball would.

It was Kobe, and he wanted to chat. We'd met weeks earlier, crossing paths in the lobby of a Scottsdale, Arizona, hotel. We knew many of the same people but didn't exchange numbers. He was currently out of action with a sprained ankle but expected to receive clearance soon to resume his on-court workouts, and he wanted to connect to work on his game. In particular, he wanted to develop two additional moves: a between-the-legs crossover made famous by Tim Hardaway, and a one-handed crossover used often by Dejan Bodiroga, a Euroleague fixture from Serbia and mainstay of his country's Olympic team who played from the early '90s until 2007. Kobe's reference to Bodiroga impressed me. It showed me he would turn over every stone and consider every possibility in his quest to become the best player in history.

I hid my excitement because famous people can spot awe quickly and it marks you for manipulation. I'd admired Kobe for years, ever since I watched him shoot four air balls without remorse during the last minutes of a playoff loss to the Utah Jazz. Kobe didn't give a fuck, my guys would say, and I respected his defiance, courage, and confidence.

Weather reports forecast heavy snowstorms in the Northeast for the day we'd discussed, so I avoided potential delays by flying out two days early to meet him in Dallas during the All-Star break. Once he landed in Dallas, I spent our first day together waiting for him to finish his physical therapy. Afterward, we discussed my plans.

I didn't overload him with detail. Like me, pro athletes have short attention spans and demand results, so it's better to show than tell. We would work on his efficiency with the ball, the velocity of his dribble, and the two moves he hoped to master. I also had several contingency plans, depending on what I sensed that day, taking into consideration his personality, mood, learning patterns, body language, and whatever else might affect him, such as if he'd spent a late night with friends.

Unbeknownst to Kobe, I would also use our first session to diagnose. I knew nothing of him other than what I heard from his peers and the media, and I needed to look under the hood. I hoped to assess how quickly he could adapt to our drills; whether he recalled mechanics even when fatigued; how fluidly he managed his movement; and how natural the ball looked in his hands.

We met at five the next morning, as he requested. I started with a basketball-infused warm-up, rather than wasting time having him warm up first without and then with the ball. Kobe lightly jogged, his body crouched and his torso up, dribbling the ball from baseline to baseline while I chaperoned him, position-ing myself either on the outside of his shoulder or slightly be-hind, signaling different numbers with my hands to develop his peripheral vision. The drill soon progressed to handling the ball with each hand in front, on his side, between his legs and behind his back, his head neutral and forward while reciting the num-bers I signaled and altering the velocity on the ball. He followed instructions precisely, maneuvering down the court shielding the ball from the imaginary defender with his off-hand.

We then transitioned to a two-ball dribbling drill that re-quired him to backpedal quickly, sprint forward, and slide right or left depending on my directions. He reacted to my hand sig-nals, instantaneously decelerating, then shifting his body weight in another direction while maintaining the rhythm of the two basketballs with both hands. He had the lung capacity of an Olympic eight-hundred-meter sprinter, but his legs soon fa-tigued and I noticed him rising from his crouch and not reacting to my directions quite as quickly as he had earlier.

Great players are sensitive to their engines, highly aware of their bodies and thresholds, especially after recovering from in-jury. I knew Kobe would only slow down for a reason and I re-spected that reason. Once I saw him fatigue, I tapered the intensity, length, and volume of each set unless he let me know he could handle more. We then moved to a shooting drill around the perimeter that required him to first take one dribble while pushing off his outside foot to propel his body laterally.

His physical therapist attended our session and asked that we cut the workout short because he didn't want Kobe to overdo it on his first day. Telling Kobe to go light requires the delicacy and tactics of a hostage negotiator.

"First day back, no need to rush. Plenty of time to get right," I said.

Afterward, Kobe sat on the sideline, his eyes shut, continu-ing to dribble the ball in the same sequences we had done minutes earlier. I left him alone, and later complimented him for integrating visualization to help him learn. He thanked me for the session. On our way back to the Four Seasons, I felt like Aladdin floating on a magic carpet. More than two decades after I first taught myself the game, the player who was the best in the world at the time had retained me to help him with his. To memorialize the moment, I updated my training log that morning by typing *Kobe Bryant* in bold under the category marked CLIENT.

I reflected on what I had seen earlier in the day. Hard work didn't impress me; every successful person across any industry worked hard. But his effort combined with his intensity, attention, talent, diligence, consistency, passion, commitment, mental stamina, and killer instinct astounded me. Plenty of athletes trained before dawn, during midseason and while on the road, but none whom I had worked with treated the game with such sanctity while also carrying a résumé of thirteen years in the league, multiple championships and All-Star Games, MVP awards and scoring titles, and hundreds of millions of dollars in contracts and endorsements.

It's rare, but at times I can put together periods of intense concentration, as when I overcame my usual capacity for distraction to spend fifteen hours a day in the library for three months when I was studying for the three-day California Bar exam. Kobe's mental stamina had carried him well beyond three months of cramming; based on what I had seen the last two days, I suspected his ferocious motivation and focus wouldn't wane even after twenty years.

At the end of the weekend we agreed we would connect at a later date. He wanted to rest his ankle and not overtax it too soon. I sent him a text the following week to check on him. I didn't hear back. *Strange*, I thought. So far he had answered every text immediately, even in the early mornings. I waited a week and sent another text and e-mail. No response.

Eventually he sent me a harsh e-mail accusing me of violating his confidences and said he was offended that I had sent him an invoice. He claimed a trainer he worked with had called him to inquire about our work together, and I must have been the source of that information. *Bullshit*, I thought. I had said nothing to anybody. I never did. Like him, I read *The Art of War* and understood Sun Tzu's teachings about operating in the shadows until it was time to strike: "Let your plans be dark and impenetrable as night, and when you move, fall like a thunderbolt."

As a matter of fact, over the course of those days with him, I coincidentally saw some of his marketing partners and never once mentioned I was in town with him. Whoever was in charge of his logistics had dropped the ball by selecting a facility open to other athletes and trainers, who must have disclosed our sessions to their former colleagues in Chicago to gain favor.

I e-mailed, texted, and called Kobe several times to try to clarify the situation. No response. From what I understood from his peers, Kobe didn't give second chances. I wondered whether his disappearance was an example of the ruthlessness I had heard about from my guys describing Kobe's tactics.

I was certainly disappointed that some third party had compromised this opportunity. If we had more history together, I'm certain Kobe would have ignored the gossip. But he didn't know me, didn't know how much I admired his game, and how deeply I respect the professional relationships I develop with the athletes I train.

The heavens gave me the gift of empathy, so I couldn't hate him, because I understood him. Fame bred skepticism and a lifestyle built with heavy insulation. He severed ties immediately. I wondered if it stemmed from a general distrust for people, his alleged ruthlessness, or whether he simply considered me someone looking to exploit the connection and take money out of his pocket like so many others.

Regardless, to this day I continue to compliment Kobe on his greatness. We travel in the same circles, and I always shake hands when I see him. Resentment and anger don't belong in this space. Superstars live in a world of consumption and they can quickly dispose of what they consume. I recognized this early on, so no need to add Splenda to my narrative. As fast as they can change cars, homes, clothes, shoes, and women, they could get rid of me. So all I could be was me and have faith that this was enough. I couldn't be everything to everyone. Kobe reminded me of this truth.

While I can quickly identify people's weaknesses, I can just as fast spot their gifts. I see the good in Kobe. I believe we can all learn from the ferociousness with which he approaches life and his ability to lower the guillotine whenever he sees the need, no different from a CEO who imposes a layoff of thousands of employees to improve the health of the company. I don't have to agree with his tactics, but I can certainly appreciate that Mamba's ruthlessness does have its place, especially when chasing a legacy and fortifying a kingdom.

CHAPTER EIGHTEEN

TWO BASKETS

u know right from wrong so fill each basket accordingly
#mylecture

I t was the summer of 2012, and, like the humidity in the Manhattan air, I lingered.

"He'll be here soon," I said, staring at my phone for updates.

"I hope," replied Trevor Ariza of the Washington Wizards.

Soon I heard JR Smith of the New York Knicks bang his closed fist on the locked glass doors leading into the gym. Dressed in matching everything with a luxury-brand backpack on his shoulders, he greeted me and Trevor with man hugs, then apologized for his delay.

I didn't criticize JR for his lack of punctuality. The way I see it, pro athletes like JR have achieved the American dream, earning a king's ransom to do what they love and would otherwise do for free, so maybe we should follow their protocol and reset our expectations and priorities. Nevertheless, I do impose a con-

sequence for late arrivers: barring any reasonable excuse and un-
foreseen circumstances, I end our sessions promptly and when
originally scheduled. Gym times are reserved, and coming late
simply cuts into their sessions.

To start, JR and Trevor skipped rope for several minutes,
followed by plyometric drills emphasizing power and balance,
executed from one baseline to the other. After a short water
break, we transitioned to a seven-spot shooting drill around the
perimeter, interspersed with full-court sprints. Trevor had
worked with me for several weeks during this off-season, so I
expected he would run longer and faster than JR would at the
moment.

JR's breathing soon became labored. His strides grew shorter
after each sprint. His knee flexion and hip extension diminished, which minimized his power and speed. JR paused mid-
way through his set. He walked quickly toward the trash can.
His head vanished.

I realized this was the fourth time he'd puked in front of me
during workouts: twice in Denver in 2010, once in Los Angeles
in 2011, and then today. I recommended he rest and rehydrate.

"First day back," he reminded me.

It's the end of July, dude, what are you waiting for? I thought,
and turned my focus toward Trevor.

I never want to see an athlete bent over a tin can sharing his
last meal with it. I don't want them to surrender because the
training feels impossible. But sometimes their carelessness and
lack of discipline requires accountability. The trash can is my
enforcer.

JR rested on the gym floor with his legs extended and
crossed, his arms in his lap, his head tilted to the side. He
watched while Trevor continued to sprint the length of the court
multiple times before taking shots that fell repeatedly through
the net. JR's fatigue hid his disappointment.

The aspirations he'd once revealed to me—to win championships and play in All-Star Games—didn't jibe with what I'd just seen.

JR was different, and different appealed to me.

A twenty-five-point performance at the McDonald's All American game his senior year in high school catapulted him into the NBA draft, and a few months later he was selected by New Orleans with the eighteenth pick. He could make hard look easy and easy look hard. He has the explosiveness to blow by defenders and the shooting range to keep them from playing off him; his physical gifts, youth, and skill promised greatness, but year after year he fell short of it.

A player-team relationship can be a lot like a romance. In its first stages, it is built on chemistry and potential. Both parties are smitten: the newly drafted player because he has reached the pinnacle and the team because it thinks it has discovered a diamond. The attraction is strong, at times heavy, both excited about each other. When the newness fades, the relationship is tested. The young player misses the team bus, he forgets the offense several times, he falls into a shooting slump, repeatedly misses a defensive assignment addressed during previous film sessions, develops tendinitis in his Achilles so he must spend less time on the court, eventually faces a return to action that lacks the initial fanfare, and sooner or later says something that gets blown up by the media, which causes his owner to frown. Coaches and front office personnel raise their voices, threaten him with demotions in playing time, and make not-so-subtle comparisons to other successful players his age. Patience wears thin. He can't rely on youth and inexperience to explain his mistakes, because many of the league's stars, like Bron, Melo, CP, KD, Dwight, Blake, Steph, and Kyrie achieved success while still very young.

Even at the start of his pro career, a pro athlete's age belies his life experience. Since his preteen years he has been anointed as special because of his talents. Coaches, AAU teams, shoe companies, universities, and media outlets battled for his attention. He is introduced to the culture of high-profile basketball by traveling extensively and sampling all the benefits that come with being special: sneakers and apparel issued by teams and shoe companies, special treatment at school and within his community, access to people and resources a normal nineteen-year-old at the University of Virginia would never see.

For JR, the honeymoon ended quickly. His minutes fluctuated because of his inconsistent play and effort; coaches banished him to the bench, and he could vanish on the court just as quickly as he could make eleven three-pointers. My hunch is that he worked hard when necessary and he loved the game, but everyone in pro sports has exceptional talent; longevity requires every athlete I know to maintain this intensity and efficiency over a career. It is *always* necessary. I thought I understood why JR underachieved.

In exchange for a persistent commitment to self-improvement, I would do everything in my power to help JR fulfill his dreams, which often meant holding a mirror in front of him while creating an environment that encouraged success. I arranged for him to train with other NBA stars, like Kevin Durant, Joakim Noah, and Blake Griffin, so they could see him and he could see them as peers. I hoped associating with the elite would make him feel part of the club, and this would encourage him to see his dreams of greatness as tangible.

For our first two weeks in the summer of 2011, JR never complained about the 7:00 A.M. and 6:00 P.M. twice-a-day schedule. At that time in his life and like most people his age, he enjoyed late nights and even later mornings, yet he gave me everything I asked of him: effort, consistency, and focus. For three hours each day, he shared the gym with the league's best, blurring the unspoken player hierarchy of professional basketball: (a) superstar, (b) All-Star Game reserve, (c) max contract,

(d) starter, (e) reserve, (f) minimum salary, and (g) ten-day contract. At first, he smiled with pleasure and a little surprise whenever he won in a competitive one-on-one drill. But with each
victory, the smile gradually disappeared as he raised his expectations. Soon he wore a more stoic expression while creating space
from his defenders with precise ball fakes, an extended dribble,
a quick release, and clever finishes at the rim. The sessions became more competitive than I anticipated, a consequence of pit-
ting the world's best and most self-motivated players against one
another. Afterward, he sat on the floor alongside his new peer
group, relieved he had survived the session and content he'd
played as well as we knew he could. He belonged.

After two weeks in Los Angeles, JR and I agreed to resume
our training in other cities to accommodate my busy schedule. I
flew to Miami. As soon as I landed in South Florida, I received
a text from JR that informed me he wouldn't make it on time.

Are you fucking kidding me? I thought as I recalled the conversation we'd had only days before about the importance of
consistency.

I had given my word I would carve out these few days for
him, so I felt obliged to honor my commitment. I followed up
with him multiple times to find out when he was going to arrive.
No response. I spoke with our mutual acquaintance, who assured me JR would be on his way. I waited. Nothing. After a few
days I flew to New York to connect with other clients. Enough.
He knew where to find me.

"That's Swish," other players said when I told them JR had
vanished. "Great on some days and not so great on others."

I vented to my mom. I had vouched for his reliability to as-
semble a core group of star training partners. I'd believed in him
when others had quit. I'd advocated on his behalf. I'd shaken
hands and honored my end of the bargain.

"You sound surprised," she said. "You knew what you were
getting into."

Mom was right. I knew his past body of work and the associated issues. He had moments of brilliance, but just moments.
Maybe he didn't want success as much as I wanted it for him.
Perhaps his disappearance and silence were his way of telling me
to leave him the fuck alone. He might be content just to be in
the league rather than face the uncertainty, pressure, and heartache that come with stardom. I couldn't reconcile his indifference with his lofty dreams. Why had he sought my help if he
wasn't ready or willing to chase greatness? And why did I forgive him for being inconsiderate and inconsistent? I'm not sure I
can define what I saw, but there was a definite side of JR that
was thoughtful and sensitive, and deeper than what others give
him credit for. Perhaps I realized with him, as I had in myself,
that we aren't always ready for what we want.

JR and I touched base again during the summer of 2012. He
asked about my whereabouts and availability. Despite his vanishing act the previous summer, I wanted to give him another
chance. Life boils down to a series of jump shots: Some you
make, some you miss, some you wish you'd taken, and some you
wish you hadn't. Great players move on, looking forward to the
next possession.

While he sat on the floor and watched Trevor Ariza sprint
effortlessly, I suggested to JR he forgo any remaining conditioning this day and simply shoot stationary jump shots when it was
his turn. He agreed. I hoped he'd feel disappointed that Trevor
was in such better shape than he'd been in late July, and the
memory of it would make its mark on him as indelibly as the
artwork on his skin.

"We still have several weeks to prepare before the start of
preseason," I said as we left the gym.

Trevor returned to Los Angeles a few days later to spend
time with his family while JR remained with me in New York to

train. He was prompt and responsive to my text messages those days, but he didn't seem as engaged as I'd seen him during those two weeks last summer in Los Angeles. I finally delivered my message early one morning. He sat on the gym floor, his back against the wall, his legs wide with his phone on the floor between them.

"You can tell me to shut the fuck up at any time."

JR nodded.

I questioned whether he really wanted to become an All-Star. His actions the last two summers and over his career showed me that it wasn't his priority, which was perfectly OK with me if that was OK with him. I work with All-Stars, players committed to greatness. I would have never agreed to work with him if I didn't believe he could be the same. But his choices and actions would never take him where he hoped to go.

I said his quest for stardom requires two baskets, one marked GOOD and the other marked BAD. Things that help him with what he loves belong in the GOOD basket, while whatever hinders him belongs in the BAD basket. I told him that some of the off-the-court stuff might be holding him back. If the things he does are important and necessary and make him play better, then great and go ahead. But if they don't, and he keeps doing them anyway, he's saying they're more important to him than the game he says he loves.

I leveled with him because it was time he heard it: "I never ever want to hear people talk about your fucking potential ever again. You've been in the league a long time, and since you were drafted, *potential* has been the word everyone has associated with you. Eventually talented guys that don't achieve become underachievers, and I never want to hear that fucking word used to describe you."

He nodded again and said nothing. Over the years I've learned not to gauge the effectiveness of my message by the immediate response of my audience. Sometimes words needed to marinate, even ferment in their belly till they realized they were making themselves sick. JR now lay on his back, pulling a resistance band over his heel to stretch his hamstrings. I removed two basketballs from my gym bag. We began again.

For the next two months, JR and his younger brother, Chris, who played for the Knicks' summer league team and stood a chance of making their opening day roster, trained with me. I enjoyed having Chris in the gym with us; he was a tireless worker and a talented athlete, a caring and supportive sibling who believed in his brother's dreams as much as I did. Our sessions began (and also ended) with a jump rope or a sprint or a jump or a slide. Once winded, we would begin a series of drills that varied each day, highlighting JR's deficiencies but with game context to add authenticity and purpose. We experimented with different release points on his shot. We deconstructed his movements to purposely confuse defenders. We worked on mastering a jump shot that ranged from eight to nineteen feet; a floater he could shoot comfortably off either foot; better and more efficient moves with the ball so he could attack the basket easily; balance, especially when he landed; isolation moves in pick-and-roll scenarios; symmetry so that his left and right hands became interchangeable; and strategic finishes around the basket. I hoped to create a skill set on par with his remarkable athleticism and, most important, a mind-set of invincibility. By learning to make the unreasonable reasonable, he would develop a level of belief that could carry him through every practice, game, and season. He was entering his ninth season but would just turn twenty-seven as training camp began. He could still achieve the stardom expected of him.

In every session I sprinkled references to the 2013 All-Star Game, its host city of Houston, and the pride his parents would feel to hear his name announced. We talked about the other

stars in the league, sharing anecdotes of their effort and success
to help him continue to see them as his peers. We spoke about
the life he hoped to give his family after earning his next contract. We spoke about the necessity of sifting through chatter to
find what was relevant and helpful to him. And we spoke about
the joy of the game that comes from playing creatively, a freedom gained only when he earned the trust of the Knicks organization through consistent performance and effort.

We met almost every day, in the mornings or late evenings, in
quiet private gyms so he could practice his craft without distraction. I agreed to late-evening sessions so he could play golf with
his brother earlier in the day. He loved golf. I encouraged him to
do what he loved and hoped it would land in the basket marked
GOOD. Spending a beautiful summer day sandwiched between
golf and basketball, accompanied by his best friend/younger
brother, was one of the benefits of chasing and catching his dream.

I never joined them on the greens, but happily imagined the
scene at the exclusive country clubs where JR and Chris played,
and the facial expressions of the affluent members when they
saw all the exposed artwork on his forearms and neck. I hoped
they would recognize the texture and depth of his interests and
personality. I read the blogs and columns, and I heard the
sportscasters, fans, and interviews. Most people saw him as a
talented but immature, inconsistent, and reckless kid who had
yet to learn to manage the responsibilities of professional sports
and fame—someone who had more in common with street culture than folks in his tax bracket. I doubted that people would
still think of him as rough and unpolished after meeting him in
fashionable golf attire and chatting with him about missed
putts, luxurious courses, and all the other details of an obses-
sive's game. I knew his charm would shatter the judgments
formed when they first saw him from afar. And I happily imagined him participating in what he loved and simultaneously em-
bracing his differences.

I knew JR had been suspended several times by his teams, once for an auto accident that resulted in the tragic death of his friend. But I also came to know him as a good son to a happily married middle-class couple, a loving older brother who supported his younger sibling's dreams, a young man who recklessly chased his own dream and whose mistakes were heavily documented on television and the Internet, and a devoted athlete with a renewed sense of dedication who monitored his progress at the end of every pickup game and workout.

JR improved his stamina, footwork, technique, skill, and consistency. He began to see the correlation between effort and progress. When I asked if our work helped him, he answered, "Hell yeah." I admired his commitment, especially on those days when his tank ran near empty. I admired the faith he had in himself to wager his time and effort on an uncertain future, since effort never guarantees success. I admired his decision to reinvent himself.

JR was itching to test his newfound powers. NBA games and practices were still weeks away, so his only self-assessments were pickup ball with his peers and whether our sessions became easier for him. When I asked him about his play, he said, "I felt like the best guy in there."

As preseason began, JR and I would touch base regularly. He filled me in on his performance, his effort, his health, and his interaction with his coaches, front office, and teammates. The Knicks got off to a hot start in 2012–2013, and the Madison Square Garden crowd would erupt in applause whenever JR entered the game. He rebounded, defended, and distributed the ball with the same enthusiasm as throwing down a massive two-handed dunk over a seven-footer's outstretched arms. In the last third of the season he especially caught fire, using his athleticism and creativity with the ball to slash to the basket, hoist shots from what seemed like the concession stands when defenders played off him to prevent the drive, and even score miraculous baskets with opponents draped all over him, images that reminded me of a not-so-friendly game of Twister. He averaged more than twenty-two points per game in that stretch, well above his career 13.1 mark, and had seven games of thirty-plus points off the bench, including three in a row. For the first time in ages, the Knicks were a serious contender, and JR was not just a contributor but an important reason for their success.

He didn't make the All-Star team. Instead, he won the league's Sixth Man of the Year Award. Good for many, but not for me and what I expected of him. I thought it resembled being called cute rather than pretty after all that he had done that year, and I hoped he would treat it as another source of motivation.

C. S. Lewis once wrote, "Failures are fingerposts on the road to achievement."

In the eyes of Knicks fans, JR met such fingerposts in the 2013 playoffs and the off-season that followed. He was inconsistent in the postseason, shooting and playing poorly in particular during the team's second-round loss to Indiana. The team recognized his value and gave him a three-year, $18 million deal, but then came the announcement he would require knee surgery and subsequently was suspended five games for substance abuse.

As I listened to the public rumblings, I wondered why we're so impatient when athletes stumble, especially those who've made progress and who need more time to find their way. Detours are only temporary, and a potential for greatness doesn't become greatness overnight. For some reason we become angry and dismissive when the stars we admire slip up again. We take their stardom and large paychecks as promises of a 4.0 GPA and perfect classroom attendance. But that isn't the case and never will be.

Yes, JR fucked up, and he would acknowledge his fuckup; he never promised perfect, only progress. We all get in the way of our own efforts sometimes, whether we slip up on our diet, don't properly study for an exam, procrastinate at work, avoid the gym, waste away at a dead-end job we despise despite our new commitment to change, etc.

I believe in JR and have seen what he is capable of. Is he perfect? No. Will he be? No again. But anyone who is willing to devote his life to chasing greatness—and is closer than ever before—will have moments when he astonishes us and others when he disappoints us. Over the years, JR has become one of my favorite people, players, and friends. And I have learned to give JR a hand when he stumbles while I continue to encourage him to find the road that is right for him.

CHAPTER NINETEEN

STEPH

toughness is character not punching power
#rethinkdefinitions

S trike while the iron is hot."

Did I just say that? I wondered, slightly embarrassed.

I try to avoid contrived motivational-speak, yet I dropped this cliché on the college All-American I'd just met, standing at the doorway to the Charlotte Bobcats locker room.

Stephen Curry had recently finished his amazing run through the NCAA tournament in his sophomore year, scoring thirty against Gonzaga, twenty-five against Georgetown, thirty-three against Wisconsin, and twenty-five more while his Davidson team lost to Kansas in the NCAA Regional Finals. His memorable performance widened his NBA appeal, and now he'd have to decide whether to skip his last two years of eligibility and take a leap of faith before the deadline to enter the draft.

"I still want to develop as a point guard," he said.

"I agree, and you will, but you're already sitting at the top."

Looking at his life from the outside, I saw all the things that could go wrong for him during another year of college basketball—injuries, poor play, gimmicky defenses—and little that could make his draft stock any hotter than it was right now. But Steph didn't think the time was right, staying at Davidson for his junior year before taking the plunge. I assume faith had something to do with his decision.

When we connected again a year later, it was for longer than a few seconds. He had recently relocated to Washington, DC, to prepare for the NBA draft based on the recommendation of a mutual friend of ours, Tim Fuller, Chris Paul's former college assistant coach. Steph's family came with him to the gym on our first day. My overprotective parents would have done the same, so I appreciated their involvement in their twenty-one-year-old son's life. His father stood at one stairwell while his mother sat at another, holding a small hardbound version of what I guessed were the scriptures because of the cross engraved on the cover. Every athlete I had worked with to date found comfort in the heavens, and I assumed Stephen was raised with a heavy dose of religion.

He already did everything well, probably because his father, a former NBA player, exposed him early to the game. Steph re-lied on a quick unorthodox push release, clever ball fakes, awk-ward finishes at the rim, and, like a squatter, could find open space on the court left unattended by defenders. Unorthodox players like Steph have an edge.

Think of basketball in terms of music theory. Rhythm con-sists of sounds and silence organized to form a pattern. There may be a steady beat, but there can also be different kinds of beats that are stronger, longer, shorter, or softer than others. Now consider the rhythm of a ball from the moment it leaves a player's fingers to when it ricochets off the floor and returns to his hand, and the subsequent beats created whenever the ball strikes the ground. The rhythm, meter, and beat of this dribble will change, depending on the force exerted on the ball, the movement of the feet, and the angle of the hand—like slicing a tennis or golf ball. A player can create rhythm and beat from the most ordinary movement, such as striding to the basket for a layup. He picks up his dribble to attack open space, plants his lead foot, sweeps the ball from one side to the other to create momentum, and takes one last step before thrusting his body upward—collectively, the time it takes represents rhythm, while every step toward the basket forms an independent beat, which all could change, depending on his speed and where he places his foot and the ball.

Talent and experience enable NBA players to measure rhythm and beat subconsciously and use them to anticipate their opponents' movement. Steph's unorthodoxy would be vital to his success against defenders who might move quicker or jump higher; if he could disrupt an opponent's ability to anticipate, it would gain him the fraction of a step he needed to get to the basket or free himself for a shot.

We deconstructed Steph's strengths and then showcased them in an unorthodox way, like preparing a chicken Caesar salad but stationing the perfectly prepared chicken, lettuce, anchovies, croutons, and dressing independently around the plate. He learned to alter the velocity of the ball to change its beat, shoot with either hand to alter movement patterns, and release the ball off either foot to prevent defenders from timing their jump. We focused on playing the game as expected, with proper footwork and mechanics, then as unexpected, with purposefully errant footwork and mechanics. He surprised me with how quickly he integrated the new material into his game, so I arranged for him to travel with me and train alongside other NBA All-Stars, such as KD, Melo, Joe Johnson, and CP.

During Steph's draft preparation, NBA teams called me to amass intel on his character, work ethic, and ability. I didn't see him as a typical rookie; I thought he would transition seamlessly to the league. After witnessing his father play more than a decade of pro ball, Steph was already socialized to the NBA experience. Nothing was going to startle him, not the speed of the game, egos, bank accounts, beautiful women, access to fame, or pressures to perform. More important, temptation wouldn't rattle him. He was raised with a strong religious background, and his spirituality and conviction kept him appreciative, humble, and centered on what mattered to him. Only self-restraint, courage, strength, and perspective could enable someone to say "not now" to fame, fortune, and a dream.

Of course, Steph's background meant he was different in many ways from most of his fellow first-round candidates. Steph was handsome, well-mannered, polished, and preppy. He spoke with a North Carolina twang and had the manners of a Southern gentleman. He earned good grades. He didn't ink his body with dozens of tattoos or rep his neighborhood in public. He spent his weekends at church, with family, and on the golf course. Thanks to his father's success, he grew up in and around privilege. Sounds like an amazing candidate—but some teams saw these attributes as a danger rather than a positive. They wondered about his toughness; how could he fit the part if he didn't look the part?

Physical appearance and socioeconomics don't dictate toughness. Some of the greatest players in the world weren't raised in housing projects and didn't earn technical fouls for fighting or pounding their chests after a dunk. Kobe Bryant and Chris Paul came from two-parent middle-class families, yet I consider them two of the toughest sons of bitches in the game. They compete against aggressive defenders who slap at their injuries—targeting the torn ligaments on their wrist and thumb when they release the ball or attack the basket—in an effort to hurt them, scare them, and remind them of their pain. Yet their performance hardly waned, and they never leaned on their injuries as an excuse.

To me, toughness means protecting what you love. The stereotype of the poor kid from the wrong side of the tracks who fought his way into the NBA didn't apply to Steph, but anyone who followed his progress could see how much he loved the game. It took toughness to transform into an NBA lottery pick at a small Division I program while carrying a team of overachievers on his shoulders deep into the NCAA tournament. Steph recognized the futility of trying to challenge other people's perceptions with words, and let his game talk loudly for him.

As I spent time with Steph I saw how he embraced his father's NBA legacy and accepted who he is and where he came from. His greatness comes in a different package from what most basketball people expect, but judging him on that basis would be as big a mistake as those years-ago playground players made when they dissed me because I didn't look the part. Steph's respect for and commitment to the game comes across in his idiosyncratic rhythms and a deadly shot that is all his own. He plays the game because he wants to, not because he needs to in order to help out his family; that's part of what makes him special.

And seeing Steph's approach made me a little less hesitant to talk about my own background and journey. I rarely shared my story with my guys because I was afraid my unusual route to the highest levels of the game would give ammunition to my critics. Steph helped remind me that performance wins out in the end. Other people's preconceptions can make it more difficult to gain an opportunity, but once you get your chance, it's up to you what you do with it.

Steph left me a ticket when the Warriors made their only trip to Madison Square Garden in February 2013. The game was on ESPN, and a national audience saw him score fifty-four points and shoot eleven of thirteen from behind the three-point arc, but the Warriors lost to the Knicks, 109–105 (Melo scored thirty-five and JR added twenty-six). The fans couldn't help cheering a little as Steph traded baskets with the entire Knicks team, recognizing that they were watching someone and something very special. I was less surprised. I knew Steph's capabilities and smiled when I heard their conflicted noise. Later that evening, JR texted me, "Steph's a problem."

I waited for Steph after the game. The postgame media must have bombarded him, because it took him longer than usual to shower and change. We spoke for only a few minutes because I wanted him to catch up with a few of his college friends who were in town. He gave me a hug.

"I'm proud of you. You were amazing tonight," I said.

"Thanks, man," he said. "I can't wait till next summer. I'm finally healthy to work out for an entire summer."

"You've become a star. One of the very best like we always said you would. I hope you finally see it."

"I do, man, I really do."

Toughness is as toughness does.

CHAPTER TWENTY

MOJO LOST AND FOUND

ur greatest glory is not in never falling,
but in getting up whenever u do
#confuciusknew

In the Superman saga, gold is a color that has widely divergent effects on the space refugee named Kal-El from the planet Krypton. Born under a red star, he has superpowers on earth from the physical effects of our yellow sun. But exposure to gold kryptonite robs him of those powers, perhaps permanently.

When Dwight Howard donned a Superman cape in the 2008 NBA Slam Dunk Contest, the comparison seemed more than apt. He looked like a statue carved from Ashford Black Marble come to life, with the ability to leap forty inches in the air and sprint faster than you could imagine. It didn't seem possible for someone so large to move with such power and finesse. Television dilutes the physical magnitude of players like Dwight and LeBron; to fully appreciate what they do, you have to see them in person. I like to think they both were born from a creative and daring imagination only the heavens could possess, combining world-class athletic talent with extraordinary physical proportions.

Yet in the 2012–2013 season, the gold in the LA Lakers uniform affected him like kryptonite, bringing the team's high expectations to earth with a thud. He was the marquee acquisition of the summer for the Lakers, part of a four-team trade in which LA gave up three players, including second-team All-NBA center Andrew Bynum and a future first-round draft pick.

Dwight was going to provide the inside presence while Kobe Bryant operated outside, with Pau Gasol in between and newly acquired Steve Nash orchestrating it all. The question most people asked wasn't whether the Lakers were going to win the title, it was how many titles they were going to win.

It all went horribly wrong right from the start. After an 0–8 preseason, the team started 1–4, and coach Mike Brown was fired, eventually replaced by Mike D'Antoni. Nash missed most of the first two months with an injury, not shocking for a thirty-seven-year-old point guard, and the Lakers struggled in D'Antoni's idiosyncratic offense. In late January they were 17–25, in twelfth place in the West.

Though the team rallied to make the playoffs—losing in four straight to San Antonio in the first round—everyone agreed the season was a disaster. And Lakers fans had no doubt in their minds who was to blame: the team's leading rebounder and shot blocker and second-leading scorer, who was playing center in the NBA just six months after major back surgery.

The vitriol was amazing. A fan in the stands threw a number 12 replica jersey—Dwight's jersey—at Dwight and told him, "You suck!" Fans cursed him, insulted him on Twitter, burned his jersey, and called the season a Dwightmare. And all this was for a player who returned to the court three months sooner than he was expected to, who was giving everything he could while his physical condition was probably a four on a scale of one to ten—Dwight had a five-and-a-half-inch growth removed from a disk in his back in April 2012, then suffered a torn labrum in his right shoulder in January 2013.

While his frequent smile appeared to be a sign of indifference, it really just hid his frustrations. Some people cry when they're upset, some yell, some write in a journal, and some just smile. He was dealing with serious physical issues for the first time in his life, and like most athletes he let his desire to play and contribute override the prudence and patience needed to take the time to fully heal.

Still, the negative chorus rang out all around him, combined with a difficult alpha-dog teammate and a coach with a system he hadn't expected to play in and didn't necessarily buy into. He was used to running to the block to touch the ball, not first setting ball screens in the hopes his teammates would find him later in the offense. Wherever he turned, he heard talk about all the things he couldn't do. Our task, in the summer that followed, was to reacquaint him with everything he can do.

We had to get his mojo back.

I first met Dwight through Josh Smith, one of my favorite players and people, at a pizza shop in downtown Atlanta in 2011. We exchanged contact info, and within a couple of weeks I traveled to Orlando to work with him.

I was surprised to see Dwight moving fairly stiffly on the court, something I suspected was caused by years of playing upright with his back to the basket, much of his movement confined to a small area around the rim. His heels struck the ground first when he ran, which slowed him down; he didn't always drive his knees upward, which suggested to me his hips weren't strong enough to fire his overdeveloped quads and glutes. He tended to drop the ball below his waist to create the swinging motion he thought necessary to propel his body upward when he attacked the basket. He also dropped the ball below his chest as he rotated to shoot his turn-around jumper, which left it ripe for defenders, rather than keeping the ball near his shooting pocket as he turned.

I showed him how to use his knee drive like a sprinter, rather than arm swing, to flex his knee and hip upward when he wanted to lift off the ground. I insisted he attack the basket with the ball high, away from his defender, and use knee drive to create upward force on his layup, dunk, and running hook shot to prevent defenders from swiping down on the ball.

I integrated some light defensive slides, sprints, or jumps with every post and perimeter drill designed to address these issues. Drills would never become intuitive and translate to performance if done mechanically, in isolation, without quickness and speed.

I see a lot when I attend games and watch my players on television, but much more when I'm with them on the court only a few inches away. I often have a hunch about what they can improve upon, then up close I see other things they should address. I can usually diagnose and prescribe medicine for their games, so the more time I spent with Dwight, the more I would see and the better I could help him feel.

I stole alone time wherever I could: while he was shooting a free throw at our sessions or even warming up on a foam roller. I hoped I could talk with him more than just direct him through a workout. I understood the boundaries he set; I was still a stranger even though we knew the same people, both loved the game, and both wanted him to become greater. I hoped he would soon trust me with his thoughts and transparency.

Dwight didn't need my help to become great. He already was. My goal for him was to become greater, and maybe even the greatest. Something was holding him back. Why didn't he consistently post Wilt Chamberlain–like statistics? Why wasn't he MVP each season? Why had he not won an NBA championship? Why didn't free agents flock to play with him? Why didn't he play with the complete recklessness and the "fuck you" necessary to become the greatest? I wanted answers and always read between the lines. I wasn't interested in a Band-Aid, like *Hold your follow-through at the free-throw line.* It runs deeper than that; it always does.

I wished we had connected earlier in the off-season. I needed more time to share with him my philosophy, what I call my "Idanics"—bite-size pieces of wisdom (like the chapter-opening tweets) I give my guys in easy-to-remember doses. I deliver them to my players over time when we're alone in a gym, over a meal, on a flight, on a call, on the way to an appearance, in tweets, wherever I can. I want them to hear me without distraction and decide whether the things I say make sense to them. We might talk about the need for selfishness, self-reliance, fun, commitment, childhood, faith, individual goals, and devotion. I encourage them to not act if the action doesn't make sense. I urge them to not relinquish their power, self-worth, or intuition. Without enough alone time with Dwight, I couldn't help him in all the ways I knew were important. I hoped we would connect again. I believed in Dwight.

Two years later I again found myself with him in a small gym. We had kept in touch. I had monitored his progress and worriedly watched as the small chunks of radioactive kryptonite entered his atmosphere.

His time in Orlando ended in acrimony. His Lakers tenure, while not officially over yet, was an unpleasant memory. He had missed the end of one season and the London Olympics. Surgery, followed by extensive physical therapy, kept Dwight away from basketball for six months. He'd had only a few weeks to prepare for training camp and preseason. The Dwight we saw during the 2012–2013 season wasn't the Dwight we were accustomed to seeing. He wasn't as healthy as he could be. He wasn't ready to play like he could.

Kobe Bryant said in February that Dwight cares too much about what people think. That has never been Kobe's problem, but Dwight is wired differently. Dwight listened to all the criticism because he is bright, thoughtful, and sensitive. He cared and he didn't want to disappoint. But eventually all the negativity became unbearable. I dare you to excel at work with aggressive colleagues who deflect blame, uninformed third parties reviewing your work product, and a persistent migraine that leaves you in a fetal position in the corner of your office with the lights dimmed. Work would suck. It did for him.

The public, media, and professional sports teams want to see sensitivity in their stars when it's convenient. Fans want to feel recognized by the players they worship; they want their heroes to autograph a jersey for the young boy standing beside his parents, to visit a hospital ward filled with sick children, to stay after a loss to speak with a group of fans because he recognizes what it would mean to them and the organization.

But sensitivity quickly becomes perceived as weakness when a player doesn't produce as expected, when his team loses games, when he seems affected by the criticism, and when harsh words and insults burn. Dwight gave everyone his time, which unfortunately meant he listened and heard everything. The criticism began to bore its way into his spirit. I see his sensitivity as a source of strength, as a reminder of how much he cares about people, his game, and his dream. But the sensitivity doesn't belong on the court. It made him too concerned about what others thought, dooming him to run a race with no finish line.

His close friends jokingly referred to him as Deebo after the heavily muscled character in the *Friday* movie trilogy who rode his undersized bicycle around town while acting as the neighborhood bully. I preferred to think of him as John Coffey in *The Green Mile*. The judicial system and the public relied on stereotype and Coffey's imposing physique to falsely convict him and became blinded to the sensitivity and compassion that enabled him to heal, not hurt, people. Like Coffey, Dwight was gentle and sensitive, but the culture of pro sports, with its machismo and impatience, used these gifts against him.

I knew we would improve his skill level and conditioning. I knew his confidence would grow from handling the intensity and difficulty of our workouts. I knew the game would feel easier and more intuitive after he'd worked with me. But he also needed to learn to compartmentalize his gifts. In other words, he could keep his sensitive, gentle, religious, and caring nature off the court while becoming a motherfucker obsessed with greatness on the court. It was possible: Chris Paul and Stephen Curry manage this coexistence, and so could Dwight.

The summer of 2013 was no ordinary summer for Dwight. Despite all the challenges of the previous two seasons, he was the most sought-after free agent since LeBron joined the Heat. Teams planned their budgets a year or two in advance to try to make room for him. Wherever he landed, expectations would be even greater than they had been with the Lakers.

When we first met in 2011 my intention was to help Dwight become greater. When we connected in Los Angeles two years later, my goal had shifted. It was essential for him that we find a way to push sensitivity off the court while restoring his mojo and love for the game. He had spent the last eighteen months battling more crap than the host of *Dirty Jobs*. I was excited to restart with Dwight, to see the things that happen when you love what you're doing: sessions move quickly, focus is deliberate, fatigue is temporary, happiness lingers, conversation bubbles with talk of opportunity and success, and getting to the gym becomes the first priority.

I wanted him to connect with the game in the most fun way he knew. This meant drawing him away from the basket and releasing him from the jail cell consisting of a ten-foot semicircle around the rim. Like a child banished in a time-out, he had been forced to stand erect, his back to the rim, his arms in the air, and his legs fully extended while waiting for someone to pass him the ball on offense or so he could block a shot or grab a rebound on defense.

Dwight Howard is not an offensive lineman built to protect the quarterback play after play. Dwight is a Ferrari who had been parked in the garage because teams assumed the only use for a 6-10, 270-pound player was to keep him within a few feet of the rim. They thought they knew what they were doing with him. In some ways they did, but they were turning him into Iron Man, stiff and mechanical.

We had to make the game fun again. I gave Dwight the ball and we spent time away from the basket. I encouraged him to hit reset and play with the freedom he had as a child growing up in Atlanta: dribbling, shooting, scoring, playing on the perimeter, and doing the things that had made him love the game in the first place. I knew his next head coach in the NBA would probably forbid him to do any of these, locking him down in the low post. But Dwight needed more than simply to hone his skills; our sessions were also aimed at reviving his spirit. No one wants to listen to the same song all the time. No one wants to eat the same meal or read the same book over and over. And no one in their right mind wants to drive a luxury sports car at the speed limit.

In order to reconnect with his younger, joyful self, we started the summer focusing on playing *small*. He moves better when he's lower to the ground, like a sprinter bursting off the blocks; I told him to envision playing in his daughter's dollhouse, where he'd have to bend his legs and drop his butt down low to keep from hitting his head on the ceiling. I shouted reminders like "Dollhouse!" or "Ferrari!" to remind him to play at this high speed all the time.

And I told him to ignore all those people who say he can't shoot.

"Fuck them! You can shoot. You hear me?! You can shoot!" I shouted it every day.

He'd heard over and over that he couldn't shoot, but I could see that his mechanics on release of his jump shot were good—not perfect, but nothing that needed a serious change.

He kept his elbow fairly in line, followed through, and kept his guide hand still. Were there things he could do better? Of course, but not every player is a technician.

Making a better shooter doesn't mean imposing a rigid technique so everyone shoots the ball the exact same way with the same points of emphasis. There isn't a one-size-fits-all answer; it requires understanding a player's movements, length, comfort, and learning patterns and then gently guiding him to a jump shot that feels natural and works for him.

I heard about the shooting gurus who had tried to help him in the past with his mechanics. Dwight is bright, he listens, he is sensitive, and he heard what they had to say. And the more they tinkered with his release, the more he heard the message that he couldn't shoot. If your boss instructed you to meet with twenty psychologists, soon you would start believing you actually had a problem.

Instead we focused on things other than his shooting release. We spent time on body mechanics, aligning his toes with his shoulders, his balance on the land, adjusting his hand mechanics as he picked up the ball and lifted it toward his shooting pocket, the arc on the shot—all done in the context of Dwight. I explained the rationale for every tweak and asked him to chime in. We were a partnership. I wanted his feedback. I wanted to hear from him if he didn't feel comfortable. I wanted him to experiment. I wanted him to try to shoot it close to the rim to see how it felt, then work his way out to the three-point line. I wanted him to give my suggestions a test drive, and if they didn't feel right, I would try to propose an alternative that would.

After only a few weeks I saw Dwight shoot the leather off

the ball from short, midrange, and behind the NBA three-point line. I saw him knock down 90 percent of his free throws once we readjusted some of the details and reengaged his confidence. Whenever he chopped his follow-through, I called out, "Show off!" to encourage him to hold his release until the ball hit the ground, as if he was highlighting how nice his mechanics actually were.

A few of his friends and even his agent came to some of the sessions, and they were amazed to see how consistently he was knocking down twenty-three-foot three-pointers. He wasn't going to shoot them in a game, but it did wonders for his confidence. I've found that when you let a player do the things that the world says he can't do, you push his mojo through the roof, and then you can go back and work on the things that he's more likely to do during the season.

Best of all, I saw how excited Dwight became about our early morning workouts. I saw him arrive on time every day and maintain a consistency in his intensity and effort. I saw him focus on new drills and walk through the mechanics of a drill precisely and slowly until he understood them. I saw him serious and attentive. I saw him choose the harder option whenever I gave him the opportunity to do less. I saw him smile, but only after we were done. And I even saw him spend an entire hour session skipping rope, without a complaint, because I'd insisted we would not pick up a ball until he could skip five hundred consecutive times without clipping the rope.

He trained every day. We never talked about rest days. When you love something, you find time every day because you want to. He didn't see basketball as a chore anymore, but as an opportunity, a blessing.

We spent a month together before he signed with Houston, who I figured then wanted him to work with Hakeem Olajuwon. I saw great progress with his game and his spirit up to that point. One Friday morning after our workout, we talked briefly about free agency and the media speculation that he had visited Houston to shop for a home. We laughed. Media and fans always speculate. He was learning to filter and not let things affect him.

He smiled and walked over unannounced to an adjacent court in the gym where we shared space with an unrelated basketball day camp for young kids. For the next thirty minutes, I watched him play with the kids. He gave his full attention to each, as if they were his neighbors. I saw the joy he brought to their faces with each interaction. I saw the utter amazement they felt seeing a player they admired on television stand only inches away and even remember their names. I saw the gentleness and sensitivity in each handshake. And I saw the joy they brought to him as no one asked him about contracts or money or what it was like to play with the teammate he called "Twenty-fo." It was pure. It was innocent. It was fun. It was what basketball was supposed to be. It was what basketball was when he first started.

His mojo was coming back. He was having fun again. He was on his way to greater and hopefully even greatest. As the spirit of Jor-El said to Superman at the Fortress of Solitude, "You have great powers, only some of which you have as yet discovered. . . ."

CHAPTER TWENTY-ONE

AMAR'E IN THE PROMISED LAND

u play by your rules & i'll play by mine
#religion #order

Beginning when I was very young, my family spent our summers in Israel staying with my mom's parents in their small two-bedroom apartment in the Hadar neighborhood of Haifa. We lived more like natives than tourists. We bought our groceries at the supermarket; played the Israeli lottery each week; listened to Hebrew-language programming on the Voice of Israel radio; sat at the beach nibbling on dark-purple plums, fluorescent-green grapes, and soft pita bread warmed by the sun; rode public buses; ate falafel and cactus from street vendors; took long naps after lunch; drank Kinley orange soda whenever possible; cursed in Arabic slang; hung our wet laundry from clotheslines; walked carefully along the Haifa streets to keep from stepping on the carob pods that fell from the trees; sat in the open-air movie theaters on Saturday evenings to watch American films with Hebrew subtitles; and wore sandals over my fiercest protest. (I wanted to wear sneakers, of course.)

Our mornings began early with a small Israeli breakfast of hot tea, crusty bread with white cheese, and sliced cucumbers and tomatoes. We would then head to the beach to take advantage of the early bird admission and to avoid the hottest part of the day. If I wasn't hurdling waves to improve my vertical leap, I was building sand castles. My sisters and I set up near the shoreline, our backs to the water, letting the wet sand drizzle from our closed fists. We defended our masterpieces with a barricade of plastic shovels, buckets, and soda cans. If that didn't work, I'd ball up some wet sand and toss it at the trespassers. My parents were very strict, but I was never reprimanded for protecting what mattered to me.

One day, I stumbled upon a red, white, and blue outdoor rubber basketball in the toy section of an Israeli department store. I returned to the store days later with my grandma and handed the store clerk all the shekels I collected recycling soda bottles. My grandma worried the ball would roll into the street, but I still dribbled it, alternating between my left and right hands, in the city streets, up the steep hills, through the park, until we returned to her apartment.

Fast-forward twenty years. I returned to Israel dribbling a ball, but this time with New York Knicks' All-Star forward Amar'e Stoudemire. I'd met him when he was with the Phoenix Suns, and I was working with Jason Richardson; we started talking, he suggested we get together on the court sometime, and one thing led to another. Over the years we developed a good relationship and a friendship.

Amar'e felt spiritually connected to Israel and Judaism, inspired by his mother's affinity for the religion. He had planned to visit Israel several times but had gotten derailed by retina and knee surgeries.

To prepare for his trip, Amar'e studied Hebrew with my mom. She taught him some expressions he could toss at the Israeli media. I was juggling multiple players at the time, but I agreed to join him in Israel because something about the invitation felt preordained. I was raised with plenty of religion, took plenty of family trips to Israel, spoke plenty of fluent Hebrew, and, over the last several years, wondered whether organized religion had a place in my life. I still considered myself spiritual and culturally connected, and Amar'e hoped to explore Israel with the same eye.

I had vivid childhood memories of our flights to Tel Aviv: the smell of cigarettes; multicolor sidewalls and blankets; a white sheet draped over the headrest bearing the El Al airlines logo; purple seats with an undecipherable design; full flights; foil-covered prepared kosher meals; and ultra-Orthodox Jews standing in back and near exit doors bobbing their yarmulke-covered heads and torsos back and forth, their faces buried in prayer books, their shoulders covered with a *tallit*, their left arms and forehead wrapped in *tefillin* as they prayed several times throughout the flight. Years later, traveling to meet an NBA superstar in Israel looked and felt much different. Now I was reclining in a spacious cradle seat while an attentive bilingual flight attendant brought me meals, movies, a headset, and newspapers. I slept comfortably for most of the flight, opening my eyes for a few minutes at a time to marvel at the magic of serendipity.

When I landed in Tel Aviv, a customs official boarded the plane to greet me. He drove me to a private waiting area for VIP guests. On family trips we waited in long queues to clear customs, and Israeli immigration officials quizzed us about our reasons for visiting the country even though we had Israeli passports. I now sat comfortably in a lounge, nibbling on Israeli cookies and fruit while customs reviewed my passport. The tea cookies reminded me of the ones my grandma stored in metal containers in her pantry. The fruit tasted as sweet as it had on the beaches of Haifa. The bite-size pita bread, hummus, and olives were typical of Israeli hospitality. And the modesty of the country was reflected in a waiting area that resembled that of a doctor's office. Afterward, I was chauffeured to a hotel in Jerusalem. I had never seen Israel from the eyes of a tourist. My grandma's apartment in Haifa was all I knew.

Over the next few mornings we trained at a local recreation center in Jerusalem. Its wood floor didn't have much give because the builders had laid the floor on top of concrete. The court was generally empty, aside from an elderly man on the far court busy with his calisthenics. He stared at Amar'e as if he recognized him but just didn't know where from.

One afternoon we visited the Wailing Wall, where Amar'e saw hundreds of religious Jews praying fervently while facing the sacred wall, a remnant of the one that surrounded the Temple courtyard. The observant Jews never lifted their heads from their prayer books to acknowledge the 6-10, 250-pound NBA All-Star hovering above them. It may be one of the few times in his life Amar'e went unnoticed.

We visited Yad Vashem, the Holocaust memorial. When my nephew wore a halo cast around his fractured wrist, my sister told me, "You can't even imagine how it feels to see your own kids in pain." I saw her words play across Amar'e's face when our tour guide shared stories of the brutality inflicted on Jewish children by the Nazis. A father of three young children, Amar'e rubbed his scalp and forehead with the heel of his hand as he listened attentively, and again when he heard the story of a Polish-Jewish physician who ran an orphanage during the Holocaust and was eventually sent, along with the orphans he protected, to the Treblinka death camp.

I sensed that our guide's description of the teddy bears and dolls found at the end of the war, left by children sent to the gas chambers, had Amar'e longing to hold his daughter, thousands of miles away. He pressed his massive hands against the glass to view the mountain of eyeglasses, shoes, and locks of hair belonging to Jews who thought they were stripping naked for a warm shower. He watched in disbelief the footage of corpses dumped like trash into empty ditches.

While hearing stories of the Warsaw Ghetto uprisings and Jewish partisans, Amar'e whispered something to me about how slavery in America and the Holocaust were evils that gave rise to some of the most heroic acts. He understandably related the suffering chronicled at the memorial to what was familiar to him. He paused to read the summaries of each exhibit in every room. The other visitors left Amar'e alone. It would have been sacrilegious to request an autograph or a photo. Other than the voice of our guide, there wasn't much chatter; seeing the evidence of such evil firsthand was like a kick in the stomach that knocked the words out of us.

Foreign correspondents and Israeli media called me to set up interviews with Amar'e. They seemed reluctant to take his genuine interest at face value; many dismissed his trip as an effort to court the large Jewish community in New York, where he had just signed as a free agent. I was puzzled that they questioned his efforts to educate and challenge himself, when he could easily have been home and partying like so many of his peers.

Back at our Jerusalem hotel that day, the Orthodox Jewish guests bombarded him with requests for photos and autographs. Seeing an NBA player on the streets of Manhattan happens, but seeing an NBA star in a hotel lobby in Israel never happens. The colorful yarmulke he'd bought the night before prompted their curiosity.

"Are you Jewish?" they asked.

Ughhhhhhhhhh, I thought.

This conversation was new terrain for Amar'e. He didn't know yet about the intricacies of Jewish law, that matrilineal descent dictated Jewish lineage unless someone "properly" converts to Judaism. He likewise didn't know the degree of political argument in Israel and elsewhere over the terms and importance of that definition. Amar'e innocently replied he was Jewish.

"Did you convert to Judaism?" "Is your mother Jewish?" "Did your mother convert to Judaism?" "Do you practice Judaism?" "Do you keep kosher?" "Why do you wear a yarmulke?" "Do you intend to raise your children Jewish?" "Do you intend to have a bar mitzvah?"

The questions flew fast and struck me as invasive and irrelevant. Why is anyone's personal and spiritual relationship with the heavens a matter of public interest? Amar'e had come to Israel out of respect for a religion and a people with whom he felt an affinity. He came to listen, to learn, and to experience. His curiosity and even his innocence were things to encourage, not pounce on and cross-examine. I was uncomfortable watching a religious community that traditionally advocates piety, humility, compassion, and respect instead poking and probing to determine just how Jewish he really was.

Amar'e took it all in with equanimity and bemusement. He had spoken from the heart and wasn't worried about the interpretations of others. He continues to identify Judaism as an aspect of his spirituality, whatever Jewish law might say about how "real" that is. His intentions were honest and his heart pure.

The whole discussion reminded me what I didn't like about religion: I don't want anybody else telling me what to do and how to live. To me that's not righteousness, it's just bullying in the name of God. I had seen it all my life, back to when I'd ask my parents if we could go to the mall on a Saturday, and they told me we couldn't, because if someone saw them there it could jeopardize their jobs. I understand the need to avoid the appearance of impropriety—but what was the impropriety in getting a salad on a Saturday at the mall?

In my sand castle, it matters more what's in your heart than what rules you follow.

CHAPTER TWENTY-TWO

A DIFFERENT STAR

if u don't fit the part, change the job description
#grace

I n the spring of 2004, I received a phone call from a gentleman named Derrick who served on the board of a friend's nonprofit. Derrick hoped I could train his teenage son and daughter. At the time I didn't have much room in my schedule, but he asked me to reconsider and I decided I'd at least meet with them. The chance to help someone fulfill their dream of playing college basketball resonated with me more than I wanted to admit at the time.

We met early one morning at the private high school his daughter attended in Washington, DC. The facility was cavernous, with multiple basketball courts, a running track, weight room, even a rock-climbing wall. Derrick shook my hand firmly and introduced himself and then his daughter, Grace, and his son, Max. Grace was in ninth grade; Max was a senior. Derrick spoke proudly of their commitment to school and sports. He struck me as a devoted father, since he'd already jumped through so many hoops just to ask a stranger to evaluate his children's basketball aptitude and ability. I took note of his monogram-collared shirt, his children's expensive private-school education, the summer vacations in Cape Cod, Duke football, Columbia Law School, and a partnership with a global real estate company; it all suggested he excelled at anything he put his mind to. Success brought money, and money bought access and resources.

Unfortunately, money can't guarantee a place on a Division I basketball team for either of his children, unless they were equally determined.

The next ninety minutes resembled a training session with any of my elite professional players: a series of drills that took shooting and ball-handling and paired them with heavy conditioning. I didn't adjust the drills or my intensity, just my volume. Max and Grace listened carefully and did their best to mimic everything I demonstrated, even though they also fumbled the ball, missed shots, ran slowly, and caught their breath whenever they could. Their effort on the first day reminded me of the kids I'd coached at the YMCA a few years earlier.

Afterward, I spoke with Derrick. I thought Max could potentially walk-on at a Division I university; he was a good athlete with good size and good grades from one of the best scholastic high schools in the country. But it was already late in his high school career, and I didn't sense that he loved the game as much as his father hoped. I also wasn't convinced that Max would trade his free time just to be a practice player.

As for Grace, she was built like her father: tall with a strong base and upper body. She was slow, with average conditioning and skills. But she tried to mirror carefully whatever I suggested and surprisingly wasn't discouraged with how many deficiencies I spotted in her game. Experience taught me to never underestimate love; it had a way of creating overachievers.

"Grace could play major Division I college basketball," I told Derrick. I didn't share with him what I saw beneath his daughter's insecurities: Grace had something special, though I couldn't yet define it.

I met with Grace a handful of times over the next few months. Our inconsistent scheduling kept us from making dramatic physical changes, but we had ample time for her to rethink her idea of hard work. She knew about my work with professional athletes, so I symbolized to her the idea that maybe her dreams weren't as crazy as other people thought. Dreams become more believable when you can touch them.

"Why do you think I agreed to help you?" I asked her.

"Because you believe I can play at Duke," she said.

There it was in a word: *Duke*. That was her dream, to play Division I ball at the school where her father had been an All-Conference linebacker.

She was right that I believed she could do it, but fulfilling that dream was going to require some heavy lifting. Duke was then in the midst of five straight years making it to the Elite Eight of the NCAA women's tournament. Grace attended a small but prestigious all-girls private school known for its academics, alumni, resources, campus, tuition, and Ivy League graduates; none of its athletes had ever earned a Division I basketball scholarship. She played in an uncompetitive basketball conference, so she wasn't likely to see coaches from Duke, Connecticut, Tennessee, Baylor, and Stanford attending her games.

I could relate to nearly every detail. We both attended small, largely homogeneous private high schools with academic credentials but little experience in the Division I basketball world. Nevertheless, we were consumed by our dream of playing college ball at the highest level.

I didn't want Grace to fall short of her dreams, so I offered her what I wished I'd had at the same age: wisdom, guidance, and resources.

One morning I arrived at the gym with Alana Beard, who'd starred on Duke teams that went to back-to-back Final Fours. I wanted to give Grace an up-close look at the effort and talent of the player whose photos Grace had posted on her bedroom wall. I didn't make any concessions for her age and ability as she and Alana trained together for the next hour.

"I sucked today. I am so embarrassed," she told her father afterward.

Humility was an amazing source of motivation.

"Yup. Very average," I said.

"I am so embarrassed, absolutely embarrassed," she repeated.

She waited for me to respond. I didn't.

I hoped she didn't consider me the gatekeeper to her dreams. I wasn't. Those were in her hands, not mine.

The heavens intended us to meet for other reasons. For her, I represented what she needed, spiritually and physically, to achieve what she aspired to. And she let me live vicariously, participating again in the sheer euphoria of chasing a dream, and to be the mentor I wish I'd had.

Several weeks later I reconnected with Grace. Her father didn't escort her to the gym this time.

"I'm ready," she said.

And "ready" meant she would eat sensibly and monitor her weight even when her classmates devoured food from the cafeteria, vending machines, and off-campus convenience stores. She would jog with weighted vests, skip rope, and run timed sprints from baseline to baseline before and after school. She would follow the shooting and ball-handling drills I recommended. I admired her commitment in the face of teenage pressures to conform. She didn't look, think, or dream like her friends. I imagine she felt alone, but that's the cost of doing business with the heavens.

As she improved, so did her exposure. She became the starting point guard on her AAU traveling team, which she helped transform into one of the best in the country. The summer circuit enabled her to play against the top players from her age group. When the school year began, she took on a dominant role on her school team and in her conference.

The following summer, several midmajor Division I programs made scholarship offers. She didn't commit, hoping Duke would eventually call. She felt pressure. I understood. The situation reminded me of waiting for graduate school acceptance or a job offer from your first choice with several other offers already in hand. I knew that delaying could cause each midmajor college program to pull its offer and give her scholarship to someone else.

In the meantime, she planned to attend Stanford's annual summer basketball camp. I reminded her to treat any time on the court in front of college coaches like final exams. We ramped up her training prior to the first day of basketball camp.

I didn't hear from her during the week of camp. I hoped it went well. Several days later I received an e-mail from Derrick and then a follow-up call. Grace had played well with the campers during her first day. The Stanford women's basketball coaches invited Grace to play pickup with the team and camp counselors later that evening. She drained shots, defended aggressively, and generously distributed the ball while the head coach for the women's team watched. And then the heavens pressed replay, because the same thing happened the next evening. The following day, the head coach summoned Grace to her office. She offered Grace a scholarship to Stanford contingent on the admissions office reviewing her grades and standardized test scores.

I imagine Derrick broke down when he heard the news. His daughter had persevered despite the reality that she could land many feet short of her dream. A lifetime of effort came down to a few days at a summer basketball camp that earned her a major Division I scholarship—contingent on Grace continuing to play well, earning high SAT scores, and maintaining her GPA.

Grace cleared each hurdle. She earned and accepted her scholarship (she never heard from Duke). She played four years on varsity at Stanford.

I find her inspiring. Grace's dream may have been to play for Duke, but as she reached for that star with purpose and determination, she had faith the game would transport her somewhere special. And so it did. Everybody can touch the stars, but it may not be the star they expected.

CHAPTER TWENTY-THREE

JOY IN THE STREETS

hand children a penny & watch them play 4 hours;
hand adults a penny & they'll toss it away
#genius

'm sometimes asked how long my training sessions go.

"A while," I reply.

Training isn't confined to a gym. It can mean late nights at home taking notes, eyes on the television during a player's West Coast road trip; responding to the flurry of text messages after a shitty game; reminding them to do what's in their best interest; reinforcing the principles we spent an off-season refining; listening when frustrations bubble; offering advice when their personal lives hit a rough patch; lifting spirits on bad days and humbling egos on good days; sitting in Tibetan silence on long flights and car rides because they wanted company, not conversation; attending their birthday celebrations, weddings, and guest appearances to show my unwavering support.

In other words, training isn't only about basketball. Sometimes it's not even about training.

The 2011–2012 NBA season didn't start as usual, when the leaves had begun to turn colors and sweaters subbed for T-shirts. The NBA chose to postpone the season until a new labor agreement could be negotiated. At issue, among other things, were guaranteed contracts, the lengths of contracts, and the salary cap.

The league prohibited players from participating in organized team practices, training at their team facilities, and communicating with the teams. Needless to say, there were no NBA paychecks for the players. Unless your last name is Gates, Allen, Jobs, or Wynn, it hurts to miss a paycheck. Every few weeks, the commissioner canceled another set of regular-season games. After each announcement my guys went AWOL. I imagined them sulking at home, in the dark, on the couch, in their underwear, the remote in one hand and some gluten-free cookies in the other. I listened to them vent when they resurfaced days later, but I wasn't completely sympathetic.

"Trust me, there's always a rainbow after the storm," I said, speaking from experience.

The recession affected everyone, and now its remnants had touched the privileged playing professional basketball. Yet it also offered some clarity. Imagine that you're dealing with some hardship at home, and a surprising colleague from work—someone in another department on another floor—is the only one who checks on you regularly. Players learned who and what mattered very quickly when the thing they loved was ripped from their hands.

The lockout even imposed a dose of modesty and sensitivity, something famous athletes lose because they have access to everything. I often asked them why they needed so many cars, bedrooms, and shoes when they could drive, sleep in, and wear only one at a time. I hoped the time away from the game would remind them of the need to save and savor.

The lockout gave them the gift of normalcy and time, two things they never have enough of. They could be normal dads. They could rouse their kids in the morning; prepare their breakfast; chauffeur them to school; attend their practices, games, and parent-teacher conferences; help with homework; celebrate birthdays on the actual birthday; escort them around the neighborhood on Halloween night; run errands; and carve the turkey on Thanksgiving. And as for time, they had more of it to train, rest, and rehabilitate lingering injuries.

Some took advantage of it and others procrastinated. I worried their training routines could grow stale with no start date for the season in sight. To keep things fresh, I gave training a different skin whenever it made sense.

It was now November. I met Chris Paul at Melo's apartment in the early morning on a Saturday. Seeing Chris and Melo dressed in all black instantly reminded me of the lyrics "all black everything" from Jay Z's "Run This Town." Years ago I would never have connected clothes and hip-hop, but these days it was my new normal. We stretched in the living room. Melo's young son, Kiyan, dressed in his Spider-Man pajamas, mimicked his father and Chris as they wrapped elastic bands around their heels and pulled to stretch their hamstrings. Like father, like son. Kiyan was part of our team.

We weren't going to the gym or to any kind of specialized training facility. It was a nice autumn morning, and we were going for a bike ride.

I had my bike with me, so Melo took his out of the storage room in his building and together we walked our bikes to the shop around the corner to rent one for Chris. We took the bike path that runs parallel with the West Side Highway all the way to Battery Park. We alternated who would lead and who would draft. I decelerated when I saw a metal structure along the path that resembled monkey bars but was probably intended as decoration. It looked tall enough and strong enough to withstand their weight, so I signaled for us to stop for a few sets of push-ups and pull-ups. We then continued to ride. The oncoming runners and cyclists were either too labored in their breathing or too consumed with their pace to notice the two NBA superstars quickly approaching. And if they did notice, within a few seconds we were a hundred yards down the path, which deterred fans from chasing after us for autographs. We even did some sightseeing, taking photos and reading the inscriptions engraved on the memorials and statues near Battery Park.

To circle back in the direction of Midtown, we left the comforts of the bike path and rode the city streets. Our heads swiveled as we slalomed carefully among the pedestrians, parked cars, potholes, and traffic. Their anonymity disappeared at the intersections. Drivers and their passengers would look in our direction, then pause with disbelief when they saw the superstars, feet on the ground, straddling their bicycles.

"Ohhhhhh shiiiiittttttt!! That's Melo and CP!" they shouted as they pointed in our direction.

Chris and Melo flashed them peace signs, then pedaled ahead.

We rode for a few hours. World-class athletes don't fatigue during a three-hour scenic bike tour ridden at a modest pace, but that wasn't the idea. The real purpose was to connect them with their childhood: the bike rides in the neighborhood with their friends, pedaling as hard as they could, gripping the handlebars tightly and lifting their backsides off the seats to help them churn the pedals to climb the steep streets.

Chris and Melo play a child's game within adult parameters. I understand why players lumber to practice, to the weight room, to morning shootaround, and to treatment, their heads covered with their team-issued hoodies. They play eighty-two regular-season games paired with practice, travel, treatment, and mandatory public and media appearances. The pressures associated with the sport seemed to convert the game they loved as children to something they could sometimes hate as adults. Inevitably, the pleasure they had always found on the court becomes overshadowed by things like labor disputes, contracts based on performance, scrutiny from the public and media, confrontational and insensitive coaches and front offices, lingering injuries, and unsupportive teammates. The game in the NBA wasn't the same one they grew up with and played on the blacktop from early in the morning till late evening.

I hoped our ride could, in some small way, reconnect them with the freedom, recklessness, innocence, and single-mindedness only children seem to have in pursuit of fun. Strip all the crap from the game, and even the most jaded pro should find fun at its core. I zeroed in on fun and the magical feelings associated with it. My job on this day was to help two ultratalented, ultrawealthy celebrities remember that magic and recapture it so they could channel it into their own efforts when it was time to get back on the court. For a few hours they were kids again, each pedaling as fast as he could, racing his best friend while hurrying to be home before dark and just in time for dinner.

How long does training take? That's a question you don't ask when you're having fun.

CHAPTER TWENTY-FOUR

ROLLIN' WITH THE KING

kings r born, rulers r made
#reigningjumpshots

At thirty-five thousand feet, the clouds looked more like mist. The view perfectly accompanied the quiet hum of voices, mostly from the guys at the back of the plane sitting in vanilla-colored reclining chairs and playing a friendly card game on the faux-granite table separating them. We were all here on this private jet because of our association with the tall gentleman napping on a nearby foldout couch: LeBron James of the Miami Heat.

The cold air from the overhead air-conditioning vent caused me to wrap around my shoulders the brown velour blanket the flight attendant had issued me when I'd boarded the plane. I slid the headphones off my ears so they rested on the back of my neck, and heard the attendant ask if she could get me anything.

"Sure," I said. "Can I have a sandwich?"

"Of course. What kind would you like?" she asked.

"Turkey on wheat with lettuce, tomato, and mustard if you have?"

"Absolutely. Anything to drink?"

I pointed to my bottle of water. She nodded. She took a few steps toward the front of the plane. She stood in front of a kitchenette and began to prepare my sandwich. She turned her head in my direction.

"Would you like potato chips?"

"No thanks. I'll take a banana if you have them."

"Sure thing, sweetie."

I suspected the answer would have been the same if I'd asked for acorn-fed Iberico ham with cave-aged Gruyère and heirloom tomatoes on San Francisco sourdough bread. Private jets are made for pampering.

It took her just a few moments to plate the food and place it before me, and then she walked back toward the card players. After I ate, I slid the headphones back on, switched on the noise cancellation, and I too napped.

When I awoke about an hour later, I could hear LeBron, one of his managers, and his business associates laughing as they told a story. Only LeBron's private security still slept, reclining in his seat, arms crossed, legs stretched out, catching up on a few hours after a long night keeping an eye on everyone.

My new normal had become traveling with LeBron James on a shoe company's private plane. "You're rollin' with the King," as a Nike executive once described it. Except, of course, I knew there was nothing normal about it. These were the moments in my life that inspired the questions, How did you do it? What's the secret?

The truth is I never imagined I would end up here twenty-five years after I first picked up a basketball and fell in love with the game. Surface appearances made it seem all the more improbable if not laughable. The players and I didn't look the same, act the same, talk the same, grow up the same, or live the same. Yet our lives had intersected and we understood one another.

Their dreams had started just like mine, with a bounce of a ball at some playground in some neighborhood years ago. After that, our faith and love in the game transported us somewhere magical. By our own very different paths, we turned a child's game into our personal fountain of youth. We chased dreams sensible men called ridiculous.

And somehow it didn't matter that I had never played or coached in the pros or even on the college level, wasn't part of a famous basketball family, and had grown up in a culture that considered sports something unfit for serious people. I had tried to turn my back on the game and pursue a more sensible life, but basketball's siren song was stronger to me than someone else's idea of "normal."

I had seen LeBron a few times over the years since that workout with Chris Paul in New Orleans, but the subject of training never came up. Then in the summer of 2011, out of nowhere, he sent me an e-mail inquiring about working with me, followed shortly by calls and text messages from CP, Melo, and a senior officer at Nike. CP and Melo explained that Bron wanted to train with me and he'd called them to get their blessing; he knew they were my guys for many years and he didn't want to interfere with their relationship with me or his with them. I really respected LeBron for that; it was a very thoughtful gesture, and I appreciated how he went about it.

We got together in person in Las Vegas on a trip to celebrate Chris Paul's upcoming wedding, sitting down in the living room of his massive hotel suite to coordinate our off-season schedules. His first season in Miami had ended in disappointment, losing in the Finals to Dallas, and he hoped to make changes in his game and approach.

We talked for a while, and I told him it would be dishonest for me or anyone else to claim they could make him great. He was already great. I was just a facilitator, there to support him any way I could in his efforts to become the greatest ever. He set his phone on the table and listened when I compared his game to a bicycle in the Tour de France. World-class cyclists minimize aerodynamic drag by reducing air pressure and direct friction. Their teams design and build brilliant bicycles while devising training protocols to shave milliseconds from race times. Only a great cycling team wielding a stopwatch can detect such aerodynamic and biomechanical inefficiencies.

I hoped to streamline LeBron's game by eliminating unnecessary movement and making him even more effective without these tenth-of-a-second delays. Examples included addressing the slight imbalance when he landed after his jump shot, lengthening the effectiveness of each dribble, creating more lateral space with footwork, releasing the ball from awkward points to counter a defender's anticipation, and encouraging him to develop a go-to move he felt most comfortable with during an isolation play. He scrolled through his iPad, and we marked the dates on his calendar when we could connect.

Before we jetted off for San Diego, we spent a few days training in Portland on the Nike campus. The campus is remarkable: museum, art gallery, training facility, think tank, laboratory, and office. It's a cross between an Olympic training facility and the Smithsonian.

Bron had a long day of meetings, so I anticipated he would feel drained before our first workout. I would have preferred an early morning session so he'd be fresh, rather than after having spent hours evaluating shoe designs and reviewing marketing strategies in a corporate boardroom. Had it been someone I worked with regularly I would have gone light that day, but we had scheduled only a week and a half together, so we had to maximize our time.

We warmed up by jumping rope, not stationary like you envision, but moving from baseline to baseline so I could also integrate some footwork and agility into his movement. The rope is never easy, so it understandably winded him. Afterward we turned to the specifics I'd promised. We spent some time working on his lateral movement, trying to shift direction east and west without sacrificing momentum, speed, and the balance on his jump shot. There were also microseconds we could save on his jump shot by having him adjust where he held the ball when facing the basket and crowded by his defender. He is usually up against defenders chosen for their athleticism and length rather than merely their size—he'll blow by them if they're not—so he forfeited his genetic advantage by lowering the ball and making himself smaller. We focused on playing with the ball high, over his head and near his shooting pocket, rather than low, at or below his waist, because this would allow him to shoot quicker. If the defender raised his arm to challenge the shot or even to swipe at the ball, this would signal Bron to blow by him. If the defender kept his arms at waist level or even as high as Bron's chest, he could shoot the ball quickly, since this high jab kept the ball positioned near his shooting pocket.

"Me and Melo have been working on this for years," I said. "It takes time. Think about what he does when he catches the ball on the wing. He goes into his high jab." I demonstrated Melo's swinging motion above his head when he catches the ball facing the basket. By connecting the move with something he had seen Melo do many times, I hoped this would trigger visual memories and speed up the learning process.

A few high-level Nike executives stopped by toward the end of our session and began skipping the jump ropes we had used to warm up. It was difficult to establish the kind of isolated environment I prefer for teaching and learning, but I recognized

Bron's Elvis-like status on the campus, and these directors were sending Bron a message that we're all in this together.

Our sessions ended in the late afternoons, after which we feasted: the first night as guests for a lovely dinner at a senior Nike executive's home, and the following night at P.F. Chang's with the Nike team assigned to Bron's line of signature shoes. Bron organized the P.F. Chang's dinner to say thank you to his team.

I watched as he sought people out, remembering their names and thanking them for their effort and devotion and genuinely making them feel special and appreciated. He gave each person on the team a pair of Beats by Dre earbuds. LeBron has rockstar status, and seeing him work the room reminded me of a musician crowd-surfing the audience. From what I knew and could see of him, he was extraordinarily loyal and generous and cared about pleasing people, which inspired them to put forth extra effort on his behalf.

After a few days we flew south for his annual basketball camp at the University of California at San Diego. He moved as fluidly through the camp as he does when he attacks the basket, patient with the young campers, charming with the parents, respectful of the counselors, many of whom played major Division I college ball. One evening he addressed the campers, and then took questions, responding with savvy and good humor, laughing out loud when one youngster asked, "If Dwyane Wade and Chris Bosh were hanging from the edge of a mountaintop just by their fingers, who would you save if you could only save one?"

Bron took part in the pickup games with the counselors at night, and I noticed him integrating some of our adjustments. I watched him struggle a little with keeping the ball high before shooting over a defender who gave him little space. When he missed a couple of shots, I thought, this is why I want to work with my guys as much as possible and in private, giving them as many reps as needed until it becomes intuitive, encouraging them to make mistakes without the pressure of being perfect every time. I was concerned he'd give up on the effort to make improvements because they weren't working right away. Bron's the greatest player in the world, and I suspected he didn't want to look awkward in front of his biggest fans and followers at a summer camp. It was nerve-wracking to see him going out and playing ball before the adjustments felt completely natural and comfortable. I would have liked more solo time with him, but that's the nature of working with a global icon.

The part of him that cares about and wants to please others is also the part that led some critics to ask if he was ruthless enough to win a championship. It seems absurd today, now that he's won back-to-back titles, to remember the questions that dogged him just two years ago—about whether he had the heart and the stomach to take over the game and dominate it when the pressure was highest. He put that issue to rest against Boston, Indiana, and Oklahoma City in 2012, and against Indiana and San Antonio in 2013.

There was a great symbolic moment in the sixth game against San Antonio in the '13 Finals. Like any man who's seen his hairline recede, I can attest to the fact that it affects your view of yourself. I understand the impulse to deny it's happening; I went the shaved-head route to destroy the evidence. "Let the dream die," as my close friend Patrick would laugh.

LeBron has worn a headband throughout his career, and an online blog called *The Basketball Jones* has analyzed in great detail how the headband has risen in tandem with his hairline. Early in the fourth quarter, trailing by five and facing elimination, LeBron went up for a dunk, and Tim Duncan brushed the band off Bron's head in some incidental contact. To everyone's surprise, Bron played the rest of the game without it, and was a monster: driving, drawing fouls, rejecting Duncan on the other end, hitting a vital three-pointer in the last minute of regulation that set up Ray Allen's clutch three to force overtime. In OT,

Bron scored or assisted on all of Miami's field goals, added a steal, and the Heat won, then won game seven two nights later.

I loved seeing him playing out there bareheaded. It was the ultimate expression of *I don't give a fuck*. In that moment, I suspected he didn't care about anything external, anything superficial, anything about appearances. It was an athlete stripping away vanity, putting aside the unimportant, and pursuing greatness with a singular focus. He threw away all insecurity and ritual and superstition, stood naked in front of the world, and didn't give a fuck. I knew right then that San Antonio was finished. It's easy to make too much of symbols, but the Headband Game immediately joined the pantheon of great Finals moments alongside Michael's Flu Game, Magic's Baby Hook, and the Willis Reed Game.

A few years ago when we first met, I wondered what seeing the whole of LeBron's abilities would be like. I caught up with him during the summer of 2013 in Los Angeles, and I told him how happy I was for him. He had done what he set out to do, earned the championships he craved, and justified the monikers bestowed on him as a teenager; he was on his way to becoming the greatest, had built his Kingdom, had become a great father, and would soon celebrate his marriage to his longtime girlfriend.

Selfishly, though, I was just as happy for me and for all of us who love the game. After all, we've finally had the chance to see what 100 percent of him really looks like on the court.

CHAPTER TWENTY-FIVE

REBORN

hear every 1 but listen 2 some
#dontbafraid2questionauthority

I met Kara Lawson of the WNBA Connecticut Sun in March of 2012 at Chloe's Soft Serve Fruit Company in Manhattan, a business I invested in, after a series of e-mail exchanges she initiated more than a year earlier. The store offers a dairy-free alternative to ice cream and yogurt, which fit with the vegan lifestyle she'd recently adopted.

Her team had been using her on the perimeter as a reserve shooting guard, a spot that took advantage of her shooting skills but one for which she was a bit undersized. She told me her goal was to reclaim her starting position at point guard. I thought that was too generic and modest for her; I wondered why she didn't paint more brightly.

She had an impressive pedigree: high school All-American, college All-American at the University of Tennessee, first-round pick in the 2003 WNBA draft, 2005 WNBA champion, 2007 WNBA All-Star, 2008 Olympic gold medalist, and an ESPN analyst in the off-season. Her coaches considered her a team player because she willingly came off the bench. She never complained, fearing it would haunt her later. She turned to diplomacy and cliché to help her through important conversations, as when she scheduled time with her coaches to inquire why she was playing as a reserve when they won more games with her on the court.

All of those traits were positives from the standpoint of her teams, but I wasn't sure they were so positive for her. She followed the rules of the institution, obeyed its protocol, respected its hierarchy, and absorbed its message of team-first selflessness. After nearly twenty years in a variety of prestigious jerseys, she had trouble distinguishing herself from the uniforms she wore. She did what they expected of her, not what she expected of herself. Corporate America would have named her Employee of the Decade.

I shared this rough characterization of her career, which left her quiet, head down, eyes focused on the spoon standing upright in her dessert. In the awkward silence, I began to wonder if I had just done some damage. And then she found her voice and started to vent. It infuriated her that they considered her a role player despite her ability and consistent performances. She felt overlooked and undervalued. She was perplexed that they never asked for her opinion; ESPN employs her as a basketball analyst to offer her insight to an audience of millions, but her own team wasn't interested in what she had to say. Basketball wasn't fun anymore. In desperation, she reached out to me and even changed her diet, becoming vegan in the hope this might initiate other changes in her life.

She still had all the basketball talent and intelligence to be a superstar, but to reclaim that status would require a change in perspective. Could she embrace a me-first philosophy? I asked if she was ready to defy authority; call their bluff; listen but not agree; challenge teammates; treat her employer as an organization, not as a team, and her teammates as colleagues, not as friends; view her employment as two full-time jobs by practicing with her team and then practicing on her own; consider her goals to be as important as the organization's; remove the disguises; address her weaknesses; and accomplish what otherwise she thought impossible.

Kara couldn't answer these questions in full—but like Grace, Juan, and Alana before her, she dedicated her life to the game and made me a promise to do whatever I asked of her. I'm skeptical of promises, but she delivered it with such conviction it felt like a plea for help. As we left the shop, I advised her to skip rope and touch lines for as long as she could before our first session; otherwise, she would struggle.

And she did struggle during our first weeks together. Tears erupted from frustration and embarrassment, as her feet seemed nailed to the wood floor while she tried to skip rope; her fingers covered by thick mittens when handling the ball; her legs carrying the weight of five men while she bounded from the floor with the ball above her head; her balance as uncertain as a wobble board when refining her jump shot. She yelled, kicked the ball, and even mumbled that our sessions made her feel like she had never played the game before. She stood alone on the court with no curtain to shield her from the spotlight. *You can't hide* was the message of every session.

"You see how much time you've been wasting all these years," I said.

I wanted her to get her playing weight down to 148 pounds, which she considered impossible after playing most of her career at 165. I could see that the weight delayed her reaction time and lateral quickness, slowed her down in transition, forced her to catch and shoot because she wasn't quick enough to get past her defender—and because of all that, postponed her dreams.

"Lose at least fifteen," I suggested.

And she did, gradually over the course of the off-season and season, showing great discipline by cutting out all sugar from her already vegan diet with the help of her wonderfully supportive husband who prepared her meals, and on-court workouts twice a day, among other things. Weight loss is the easiest form of self-improvement to recognize, which is why weight-loss shows work so well on television.

She finally began to dispose of the disguise after all these years. Her commitment to self-improvement forced her to confront the demon of self-doubt. Hard as it is to imagine, she was a WNBA All-Star and Olympian who dreaded dribbling with her left hand. She favored the right side of the court, where she could lean on her right hand to dribble and pass. In the open court, she picked up her dribble early and relied primarily on a catch-and-shoot jump shot. Like soldiers patrolling for mines, coaching staffs hunt for player tendencies and weaknesses; opponents then focus on that weakness and attack with ferociousness and brutality. For Kara, it was her left hand—and, like a toupee, everyone knew, even if Kara thought she could hide it.

Basketball on its highest levels requires symmetry, each limb and side of the body mirroring each other. Developing NBA proficiency with the weaker hand is as challenging as learning to write with that hand. I insisted she perform a series of moves with her left and right hand and with precise mechanics while she maneuvered, at full speed, through a series of cones stationed close together along the length of the court—then finish with either a jump shot or layup. She repeated the drill hundreds of times until catching her breath, not her insecurity with the ball, became the priority. I shouted to stay low, torso up, focus on my hands and count my fingers; I gave different directions, sometimes frivolous ones, so she would focus on complying with my instructions and learn to control the ball unconsciously. She rarely requested rest or water breaks even though they were always available. Whenever she saw improvement, I made the drill harder, insisting she run more, faster, in less time, while incorporating a circuit of jump ropes, resistance bands, and multiple basketballs.

Her left hand gradually became her other right hand.

I laced our workouts with reminders to become more selfish. "Selfish" is overloaded with bad connotations in sports, bringing up visions of the playground gunner who shoots every time he touches the ball, the wide receiver who loafs down the field if the pass isn't coming his way, the batter who won't hit a grounder to the right side of the infield to move along a runner because he doesn't want to hurt his stats.

To me, "selfish" means being self-reliant, taking care of yourself and worrying about yourself and your family—which means taking complete responsibility for you. Don't expect your coaches to help you; don't expect your buddies to help you; be selfish in your commitment. Survival. This is what it takes. If you're completely committed to you and your development and your growth, collectively the whole team will get better. Each person's commitment raises the level of accountability and seriousness; when everyone recognizes how serious each person is and realizes what each one has sacrificed, they won't allow for any bullshit. This is why Kobe is the best teammate as well as the worst: because Kobe is completely selfish. And if you aren't as selfish as him, he'll be like, *You don't need to be here.*

The opposite of selfishness, in sports-speak, is wanting only to win. That's the crowd-pleaser, the coach-pleaser, the traditional aw-shucks mind-set that teams want to encourage. Winning sounds cool, but winning in professional sports is almost completely out of a player's control. Think about it:

Winning means the general manager and the front office are on the same page.

Winning means the coach doesn't have an ego that overrides better judgment.

Winning means having faith in the team's overall direction even when faced with losses.

Winning means knowing when to adapt even when having success.

Winning means an ownership group has the discipline to step away even when tempted to make an impulsive decision.

Winning means the team stays healthy.

Winning means guys aren't firing up shots in a contract year because their agents, mothers, wives, and girlfriends hope for a big payoff.

Winning means that there is trust all through the organization. Coaches, players, management, and the medical and training staff all trust one another, so everyone can actually do their work, do what they're best at without worrying about being undermined from one direction or other.

If all those things go right, then at least you have a chance to win. How many teams does that describe in a given year? How much control do you have over whether you're playing for one of them?

It's more useful to think in terms of the collective win and the individual win; for my guys, I'm concerned with the individual win. If they get a better contract, if they get accolades, if they improve, if they feel better, then they've won. I'm asking them to redefine what *selfish* is and redefine what *winning* is and redefine what *team* is. My players are my team. When they play well, that's our win. That doesn't mean that you don't care about your teammates. You're trying to do your best, and if collectively everybody worried about themselves, you'd have a pretty amazing team.

You don't lose games by being selfish, if that means striving to make yourself the best. Approach it like a business. If I ran a team, I'd tell my best scorer that he's my chief executive officer of scoring. That's his responsibility, his department. I'd go to my top rebounder and defensive guy and I'd say to him, "You know what my goal for you is? Defensive Player of the Year. Hall of Famer. Be the best *ever*." For the multidimensional player, be the best combination of everything. Make yourself the best outlet passer. The best ball-handler. The best pick-setter. When Kobe reached out to me that first time, I told him, "I don't want you to be great. I want you to be the greatest ever." And he understood that. But only selfish people understand it.

On the professional, advanced level, all sports teams are complex organizations filled with people trying to maximize earnings and results. Wins and losses are profit/loss statements. That's what they are. So let's run it like a really efficient company. Businesses don't demand that you put aside your own goals and priorities; they take advantage of every person's ambition and hunger. I've never heard anyone called selfish in a business context; each person runs his own department, and the results benefit everybody.

The institutions of pro sports consider this philosophy blasphemous. They don't want to acknowledge that money and individual awards are what motivate most professional athletes. Even if athletes don't prioritize winning or perhaps define it differently from the organization, this doesn't preclude winning. Winning can mean achieving individual goals. Besides, coaches and general managers say they want players who value winning over money, but they conveniently don't mention that team results are how they earn bigger contracts themselves.

Every psychiatrist and counselor in the world reminds their clients that the only thing you can control is you. I wanted Kara to embrace that message, get herself into killer condition, confront her weaknesses, and seize control of her game and her life. Athletes only have a small window of time to pursue their dreams; it was time for her to forge her own path and stop accepting her employers' conception of the right one.

Kara improved as a player and an athlete. She dropped weight while simultaneously becoming quicker, faster, and stronger, which expedited her improvements on defense and with the ball in transition and half-court. And this improvement helped her formulate new and bigger dreams. She believed she would start and again become a WNBA All-Star, the best point guard in the league, an MVP candidate, an Olympian, and a WNBA champion. She loved the game again the way she once remembered, playing with the optimism and enthusiasm of a young girl first embarking on her dream.

"Fuck them!" I yelled. "Do what's best for you!"

And she did.

In the first nine years of her WNBA career, Kara averaged 9.3 points per game, 2.2 assists, and 2.4 rebounds; shot 41 percent from the field, 39 percent from three, and 87 percent from the line.

In the 2012 season, she averaged 15.1 points per game, 4 assists, 3.9 rebounds; shot 49 percent from the field, 43 percent from three, 93 percent from the line, and helped her team to the Eastern Conference championship.

At age thirty-one, she transformed herself into the star she'd always had inside her.

The period just before the start of the season is always most exciting for me, and the weeks leading up to the 2013 WNBA season were no different. This time Kara and I had much longer than six weeks to prepare. She began our training fifteen pounds lighter than when we started the previous year, and her skill set, conditioning, and mind-set had improved dramatically.

Maya Moore, a WNBA All-Star and Olympian who plays with the Minnesota Lynx, hoped to work out with us based on a recommendation from her agent and Kara's husband. I thought it would be worthwhile to put Kara and Maya together. I could introduce more competitive one-on-one drills that would force each of them to adapt: Maya would be up against a quicker and more polished guard, while Kara would face a bigger and more athletically gifted wing.

I consider Kara and Maya two of the top ten women ball-players in the world, and I was curious to see their interaction. Like KD, Blake, and JR in prior years, Maya and Kara supported each other, clapping their hands and yelling motivational words when each looked like she couldn't handle another sprint. They offered each other instruction on proper mechanics when fatigue overwhelmed them. They talked about sharing a locker room as part of the US National Team. They even shared nutrition and recovery secrets.

After each workout we would walk to a local shop, where Kara would suggest juicing and protein alternatives to the younger Maya, who also wanted to shed some weight before the start of camp. Kara generously volunteered her insight and wisdom about the commitment a vegan diet required and her understanding of how to find proper nutrients without relying on animal-based protein. Over the next few weeks they ate, trained, and lived together. They even attended church together and discussed the messages of the Hillsong Church pastors.

I advocate self-reliance and selfishness to get ahead. But selfishness in pursuit of your goals doesn't have to create bad people, it won't necessarily disrupt organizations, and it isn't the cause of losses. Encouraging good people to be self-reliant and to focus on their success doesn't mean they lose their humanity, kindness, and generosity. You can be self-reliant and selfish without becoming completely self-absorbed.

Kara is one of the most inspiring athletes I've ever known. She showed me she could wake up each morning committed to becoming the best player she could be, and then lay her head on her pillow each night knowing she was equally committed to being the best person she could be.

CHAPTER TWENTY-SIX

WORDS OF WISDOM

ain't no right or wrong way, just your way
#noformulasostopasking

Maybe because I came late to teaching, and got here by such roundabout means, I'm very much aware that I don't know it all, that I'm still learning, still figuring things out. And sometimes the lessons come from the most unlikely sources.

I was over at my sister's for dinner. I walked up a short flight of stairs and found my niece sitting cross-legged in the living room, bent over a coloring book, a box of crayons by her side.

"What are you working on?" I asked.

No response from my young niece.

"What are you doing?"

Still nothing. I tapped her on the shoulder.

"Coloring, can't you see?" she answered, clearly annoyed by my inability to grasp the obvious.

"Uhmmm, yeah, I can see, but what are you coloring?"

"Nothing."

"How can you be coloring nothing?"

"'Cause I am."

I began to tickle her. First under her arm, then her neck, and eventually her belly until she exploded in laughter.

"Stoooopppppppppppp," she tried to yell but couldn't frame the words because she was giggling so much. "Stooopppppppp Iddddaaaaaaannnnn!" she finally succeeded in yelling.

I relented. As I moved my hands closer to her tummy in my most sinister fun-uncle way, I said, "Are you going to tell me what you're coloring or am I going to have to tickle you again?"

"An elephant, can't you see?" she said and then started to giggle. "Don't tickle me anymore, pleeeeeeaasse."

She had the page open to an illustration of an elephant grazing near a lake.

"Have you ever seen a red elephant with purple legs and black tusks? They don't exist," I said as I pointed to the page.

"Yuppp," she answered.

"Elephants are gray, not red. Their tusks are white, not black," I said.

"Ohhhh, I know that," she answered.

"You do?"

"Yeah, mommy showed me that already," she said.

She gripped the black crayon so tightly in her small right hand that she had to rotate her wrist in a circular direction when she colored.

"Hold the crayon like this," I suggested, showing her the crayon resting between my thumb and index finger.

She continued to draw as she had.

"See what happens when you don't color in the lines?" I asked, pointing to the red, black, blue, and green grass.

"I know," she answered.

"Can I show you something?" I asked as I reached for one of

her crayons. "Look, when you color in one direction the drawing looks much cleaner." I flexed my wrist up and down to show her what I meant.

"I'm fine," she answered.

"Don't you want your drawings to come out nice?" I asked.

"Yup," she said.

"Then why aren't you using the right colors, coloring in the lines, and coloring in the same direction like me and your mom showed you?"

"Because it's my drawing," she answered.

She smiled and continued to color.

CHAPTER TWENTY-SEVEN

LITTLE THINGS

we never know how much we can impact someone's life
#guardianangels

As a natural consequence of the life I lead today, I spend more time than I could have ever imagined with highly visible celebrity athletes. Basketball players who go out in public have no way to hide; a famous actor or a baseball player can put on a cap or dark glasses and go unnoticed at least for a while, but Kevin Durant can't escape being 6-9. Wilt Chamberlain supposedly got so tired of being asked, "How's the weather up there?" that he once spit on the person who asked and said, "It's raining."

Velvet ropes and VIP treatment are an unfortunate necessity for stars on this level. They have traded their privacy for their NBA dreams, and did so when they were too young to understand all the consequences. When you're a teenager and you're used to being the center of attention, you want the brighter lights, the bigger stage; it never occurs to you that someday you'll cherish the times when your life is quiet and normal like everyone else's. Those moments more often than not come behind the gated walls around an enormous home, the tinted windows of luxury cars, and the reclining chair of a chartered flight.

Money can buy privacy and some sense of normalcy, but high-energy young people can't live like hermits. They want to do all the things their age-group peers do: go clubbing, go to concerts, eat out, let loose, have fun. The biggest stars are pop-culture icons, and the adoring public wants to see them, touch them, be with them, come away with a piece of them. Most of the time, the players I've traveled with are understanding and accommodating, even after long days and tough losses, and even while they're with their families.

When I've been out with Melo over the last several years, I walk either in front or behind him so his security detail can flank him on both sides. I admire his patience with his fans: complete strangers who adore him and wait for him after games, at the mall, at restaurants, at bars, at nightclubs, at events, at the airport, on the sidewalk, at the grocery store, at the hotel, and at the gas station. They hope to say hello, to shake hands, to ask for an autograph, to pose for a photo they can send to their friends or post on Twitter and Facebook and Instagram.

One time when I knew his energy was low I asked him, "Do you want me to tell them not now?"

"Nah, it's cool," Melo said.

"You sure?"

"Yeah, it's cool."

"Why is it cool?"

"Because they'll always remember," he said.

"Remember what?"

"You just never know what it could mean to someone."

I wondered if this was a good use of his time and energy, but I left it alone. I figured we would talk about it on another day.

Before we ever had such a conversation, I learned for myself the wisdom in his words.

In December 2008, I received a call from my mom late one evening. My brother-in-law's father had just lost his three-year battle with Lou Gehrig's disease. He was a great man, father, husband, grandparent, coworker, colleague, and friend.

I left New York's Penn Station in the early morning for the three-hour train ride to Delaware. My family picked me up at the station and we drove together to the funeral service. I tried to nap in the car so I could hide from my thoughts. I wasn't prepared for tragedy. I wondered how much I would cry, how my brother-in-law and his family would fare, how my sister felt, and what I would say to them after the service. I dreaded funerals, not because I didn't feel others' suffering—just the opposite. I felt so much sadness, as if their feelings were amplified inside of me.

"Look at my score," my niece interrupted.

She and my nephew were too young to understand where they were headed and kept busy playing their handheld games. I wished I too were eight years old. We continued along the two-lane road for more than an hour before we arrived at the small church located in a small town in New Jersey. It reminded me of a church you would see in an old Western: a nondescript white building surrounded by a half acre of grass colored a dull shade of green. We parked the car in the gravel lot. We walked slowly toward the church, the pace of our strides reflecting the sadness we felt. I watched from afar as my sister, my brother-in-law, and his family arrived.

An usher directed us to our seats. My parents and I sat in the last pew in the back of the sanctuary. I stared out the window, occupied by my own thoughts: reflecting on his life, concerned about the grieving family's well-being, praying for their strength and courage, and selfishly wondering how I would handle trag-edy. These thoughts all collided and soon my lips were quivering as my tears brewed.

The service was short. Afterward, we patiently waited in line to express our condolences to the family. I was the last in line. Eventually I made my way to my brother-in-law's mother, who had just lost her husband.

"Idan, I wanted to thank you," she said as she wrapped her arms around me.

"You don't have to thank me," I said. "Rain, snow, sleet, hur-ricane, blizzard, tornado; I wasn't going to miss this."

She smiled. "I wanted to thank you for what you did . . . the tickets to the Masters."

A couple of years ago, after doctors had first diagnosed her husband's debilitating disease, he talked about his dream of one day attending the Masters Golf Tournament in Augusta, Geor-gia. He loved golf. The Masters is one of the most popular sporting events in the country, and the tournament sells out completely, mostly to ticketholders who have held the privilege for generations. There is a so-called secondary market of brokers and buyers, and tickets can cost a fortune. I called a few people I knew who could potentially help out, and eventually, with ev-eryone's help, we found two passes to the tournament for him and his wife.

"Yes, I wanted to thank you so much for the passes to the Masters. It meant so much to us."

"You are very welcome. I'm really happy you were able to go."

Then she grabbed my hand. "Idan, thank you for *more* than the passes: Thank you for what you did."

I paused. I looked at her. She could tell I didn't understand.

"We walked to the Masters Pro Shop on the second day of the tournament. A Masters shirt caught his eye. He walked over to the aisle and unfolded the shirt. I saw him lift the price tag from inside the collar and then rest the shirt back on the stand.

'Get it,' I said to him. He thought it was just the coolest shirt, but he thought the hundred-dollar price tag was too expensive. I insisted he buy it. He looked at me and I insisted again, so he picked up the shirt and walked over to the counter. The disease had begun to overtake his motor skills, so he wasn't able to smile, but I knew how excited he was to have the shirt.

"To make a long story short, Idan, I buried him in the shirt. Thank you for touching his life. You gave him his dream."

I burst into tears.

Melo was right. You never know how big a small gesture can be.

CHAPTER TWENTY-EIGHT

FROM THE PERIMETER

does greatness allow u 2 follow your own voice,
or does following your own voice make u great?
#chickenoregg

One afternoon a career ago, I was sitting in my colleague's office chatting about everything other than the
law when his supervising partner knocked. She looked concerned as she held his legal research memo in her hand. She
wondered if he could have reviewed more material. He smiled,
pulled open his desk drawer, looked inside, raised his head, and
replied, "I also didn't look in here, but I know what I gave you is
correct." That was it. He trusted his voice. It's what made him
special.

I could never have gotten away with that.

For most of the players I work with, that kind of confidence
is as natural as breathing. They are the elite of the elite, and they
expect the world to bend itself to accommodate them. Before a
game you'll find them perched in front of a locker, bobbing their

heads to the music pouring through some oversized pair of headphones; the ritual helps them focus and minimizes the external chatter that inevitably surrounds them—from the coaching staff, athletic trainers, strength coaches, physical therapists, front office, family, friends, teammates, agents, managers, personal assistants, shoe companies, media, fans, etc. Everybody has an opinion and advice—run the offense, play smarter, work harder, run faster, play under control, be tougher, learn quicker, don't hang out, arrive early, dribble less, foul less, pass more, shoot more, shoot less, and on and on. It all bounces off them, as it should. Great players follow their own voices.

But while every player in the NBA is great—maybe not great at everything, but special in some way or else they wouldn't be there—they can't all headline the music video, dancing to their own beat at the same time. With very few exceptions they were all incredible as they were learning the game growing up, starring on their scholastic and collegiate teams, heavily recruited and infused with a strong sense of their own worthiness. Making it to the NBA is the fulfillment of a dream.

It can also provide some hard lessons about your place in the pecking order.

I first met Wesley Johnson in the summer of 2012, at the urging of his older brother and the GM of the Minnesota Timberwolves. The T-Wolves took Wes with the fourth pick of the 2010 draft, and they were expecting great things from him. The results hadn't matched what they'd seen from him in college. In more than two thousand minutes of play in his rookie season he averaged fewer than ten points per game on less than 40 percent shooting, and his minutes and production both went downhill in his second year. Minnesota was facing a decision on whether to extend his original deal, and they wanted me to see if I could help him rediscover the talent and confidence he'd displayed for Syracuse.

Before getting together with Wes, I watched a few YouTube clips of him from college. I could easily see why he'd gone so high in the draft. He was 6-7, with elongated arms and legs, a narrow waist, and broad shoulders, all of which reminded me of the characters in an Ernie Barnes painting. His athleticism was off the charts. He could run like the wind and jump to the moon. If he hadn't pursued a career in basketball, he could have developed into a world-class sprinter. He once told me he ran the two hundred meters in the Texas state championships as a high school sophomore without ever practicing. Let me translate: He ran and starred in track meets as his excuse to leave class early.

I was just as impressed when we met in person. He has an easy Texas charm, along with good looks and manners. He had barely touched a ball since the last game of the season, yet his conditioning was still strong, he made shots, and the ball looked comfortable in his hands. Great players don't regress dramatically even when they go without practice for a while. Everyone else needs a little time to recalibrate their distances to the basket, the feel of the ball and its weight, the rhythm of their dribble, the length of the court. Not Wes. He had *it*. I could see what was tantalizing and frustrating about him.

After several days of our working out together he had to rush home because his pregnant girlfriend was about to give birth to twins. I assumed we'd continue with the sessions once he got somewhat settled into the routines of fatherhood, but we didn't. The next thing I heard was that he'd been traded to the Phoenix Suns. I thought the change in scenery might spark him, but it didn't. His minutes fell even further, down under a thousand. His scoring per minute was up, but the last-place Suns felt they'd seen enough and let him become a free agent after the 2012–2013 season.

Now two teams had given up on him, which puzzled me, but I had only spent a short period of time with Wes. The Wolves and Suns had each seen him over a full season. Talent and fireworks on a few random nights in December aren't enough; succeeding in the NBA requires consistency over an extended period of time—eighty-two regular season games, six months, a daily grind.

He reached out to me again at the end of the 2012–2013 season. I agreed to see him, to try to hit reset on his career and help him land a new spot somewhere else where he could still achieve his potential.

On my way to the gym to see him for our first session I reminded myself to have patience with him, because others clearly had lost theirs. All the physical ability was still there—the speed, the hops, the conditioning. He still had the Scottie Pippen–ish body, the ability to put the ball on the floor and attack the basket, a good shooting touch, and he could take off from either leg and soar. He was the kind of scoring swingman teams are always looking for. What was holding him back?

We spent a lot of time talking: about pro ball, the NBA life, managing personalities, and juggling the competing interests of players and teams. He felt like he couldn't play with any kind of freedom, that he found himself questioning every shot he took. Coaches wanted him to be a spot-up shooter, to find somewhere on the perimeter and wait for the ball to come his way. This left Wes feeling handcuffed; he had risen to the pro level because of his athleticism and talent, and now teams were telling him that wasn't what they wanted. What did they want? And did they really want it from him?

I encouraged him to be open with me, listened, and acknowledged his frustrations. I wanted him to reconnect with the guy who had been Big East Player of the Year and a first-team All-American, who smiled while he played, shot without hesitation, attacked the rim, and then pulled on his jersey proudly as if to say, *This is who I am.*

At the same time, Wes wasn't yet an All-Star and Olympian like Kara Lawson being pushed into a diminished role before she was ready for that, or Dwight Howard trying to reclaim a position at the very top of the player pyramid. This was a high draft pick facing a career crossroads: accept that his best chance of staying in the league at the moment was to reinvent himself, or else prepare himself to chase the game in Europe or China or other foreign outposts.

Some people in the league questioned whether Wes cared enough, whether basketball was important enough to him, whether he loved the game. From their perspective that's the ultimate sin, but in human terms I wouldn't fault him if he didn't. We push gifted people in the direction of their talents all the time, and they end up doing something we believe they should do instead of what they want to do. I wanted Wes to show me his answer, even if that meant basketball fell fourth on his to-do list. I needed to see whether he treated each training day with the same enthusiasm as he did our first; whether he needed an excessive warm-up because fatigue and melancholy had substituted for adrenaline; whether he used rest breaks to rehydrate or to check text messages; whether he reserved our conversations for all the complexities associated with the game or for everything else; whether the disappointment of under-achieving really stung; whether he could motivate himself; and whether he could climb out from his self-inflicted Grand Canyon.

The first few days of our training reacquainted him with my definition of effort. All athletes talk about hard work; they all talk about "grindin'." Commercials celebrate the guy who always does more, never stops, pours sweat, and keeps on working. It's a cliché and it's meaningless; in sports, hard work is assumed, and results are what matter. Can you work efficiently, productively, in a way that hones your performance and gives you an advantage? It's not about the hours; you can take eleven hundred shots and be impressed with your effort, or you can take five that are done in a way that mechanically makes sense to you, and with the speed, focus, and intensity that mirror the action of a game, to create the neural pathways necessary to produce under pressure. From the beginning, Wes responded to our sessions with an admirable openness, internalized the lessons, and came back for more. After a few weeks I put a check mark by the words *love of the game.*

There were technical things for us to address. He leaped very high on his jump shot, which caused his shoulders to rotate away from the basket. It's hard to jump high without swaying, and he had trouble landing in perfect balance, feet striking the ground softly and at the same time, shoulder-width apart, which meant that he was not in balance when he released the shot. He didn't need to jump so high on his release; he could create space with a quick jump and even quicker release. I suspected this flaw was tied to his physical gifts—he loved to jump high because he could, but on his shot it was counterproductive. I suggested he save his best leaps for when he's close to the basket, and we worked on controlling his jump when shooting on the perimeter.

In the open floor, he compromised his own speed by taking too many dribbles. He needed to learn to push the ball out and sprint to retrieve it; I had him stand on the wing parallel to the midcourt line, passed him the ball, and told him how many dribbles he was allowed to take before finishing with a dunk or a layup. I also noticed that he tended to land very heavily when he came to a jump stop, which meant he couldn't use his momentum to change direction fluidly. We worked on landing softly and quickly near the ball of the foot so he could explode forward. We corrected the release point of his shot, keeping his right elbow pressed firmly to his right side and his left hand guiding the ball to the right side before he released it; I told him to visualize the barrel of a gun, held with the off hand and pointed at the target. To help his lateral quickness, we skipped rope every day; like many players with incredible forward speed,

Wes didn't pay enough attention to lateral movement, preferring to do the running and jumping he'd always excelled at.

As he improved, I could see Wes getting more frustrated when he made mistakes. I thought this was a great sign. He was demanding more of himself, not tolerating sloppy efforts, and reacting to his current situation with the urgency it required. I loved it when he yelled, kicked the ball, even tossed it at the wall when he fucked up; it showed me he cared, and represented the higher standard he would have to hold himself to. It irritated him that he had to endure free agency while his peers in his draft class auditioned for USA Basketball and signed max contracts. While they showcased in Las Vegas during the summer of 2013, he auditioned for teams as if he was new to the NBA. We talked at length about his frustration. He eventually accepted that he had created this reality and it would take time to change other people's perceptions and convince them he had reinvented himself. He would have to earn the right to show his emotions and frustrations to his new employer; until he did so, they would seem like arrogance.

My parents are teachers, so I often see life lessons in the context of a classroom. I compared his play to sitting for an exam. A teacher can only grade her students based on what she sees on the paper. The same thing applied to the NBA. Wes had every physical gift imaginable combined with basketball skill, but none of it mattered if he didn't show it when he played. By the end of our month working together he understood my message of *Show your work.*

I saw constant improvement in Wes over the course of our sessions. Along the way, he had the opportunity to showcase his talents for Mike D'Antoni and Mitch Kupchak of the Lakers. I led him through some drills; they wanted to see him shoot from the outside, and they must have liked what they saw because they signed him for the veteran's minimum salary of just under a million dollars.

It wasn't what he expected when he came into the league. But it was another chance.

We talked at length about how personal goals, legacy, and winning can coexist. Each player pursuing his own greatness can elevate a team; playing a role and fitting in are not the same as wearing a straitjacket and selling out. I marvel at Wes's ability, and I hope he will be able to show his team what he's shown me. I remind him that I believe he can be great. But at the moment, he needs to initially take what the team expects of him and incorporate it into his own vision; only then will he be able to play instinctually, fearlessly, and with the right level of intelligent abandon.

The greatest players live in penthouses, enjoying the view and the luxury. They can be selfish, ignore orders, shoot without hesitation, play without conscience, talk candidly and directly with the team owner, offer opinions on personnel, create and project their own unique styles, and embrace their differences.

But nothing is permanent in the league. For now, Wes can continue to make beautiful music along with the other musicians seated in the orchestra. One day I truly hope he will again earn the right to perform his solo. At that moment, the only voice he will hear is his own, and mine cheering loudly from the balcony.

CHAPTER TWENTY-NINE

COACHES' SUITE

a suit doesn't mean ur smart
#justatitle

've usually operated on the fringes of the pro basketball world. My guys are generally among the most prominent and high-profile figures on the court, but my own role is in the shadows, which is fine with me. I'm comfortable standing a bit apart, observing, assessing, seeing ways to improve something, and having the freedom to address issues directly without worrying about political ramifications.

Being an outsider is a natural state to me. It may stem from my upbringing, being from an immigrant family in a not-so-immigrant community, Jewish in a largely Christian country, not wanting to isolate myself from the culture around me but not being wholly a part of it either. Basketball was a bridge to the world outside my community, but even there I was an outsider because of my background and the self-taught nature of my game and my skills.

When I work with my guys, my role is as both teacher and trainer—a mix that used to be embodied in the word *coach*. In the modern NBA, a coach is an organizational figure as well as a hands-on manager, at least as responsive to the wishes of the front office above him as he is to the needs of the players below. Yet everybody says the NBA is a players' league, and certainly the ability to indentify, attract, and develop the best players is the most important attribute of a winning organization.

Because I've operated outside the structure of the institution for the vast majority of my career, with my focus completely on helping my guys get better, I haven't come into much contact with the coaches around the league. I'm sure there are terrific strategists, motivators, and communicators among the few dozen individuals who hold those positions. As with any profession, some are better and some are worse; possessing the job title doesn't automatically confer judgment and wisdom.

There have been a few times when I've come into conflict with coaches, usually because they either didn't understand or didn't want to understand the nature of my efforts with my players. Those interactions have sometimes left me shaking my head about the insular nature of the institution and the people within it. The good news is that the league seems to be increasingly open to ideas and people from the outside; in the years to come, experiences like mine may be more the exception than the rule. Nonetheless, they definitely helped reinforce my own native skepticism about titles and bosses.

I. LARRY BROWN

stop knockin on doors, build your own house
#lifesconstructionproject

Larry Brown looked much younger than I expected when I first saw him stroll through the Charlotte Bobcats practice facility during the summer of 2008. I had discovered my own fountain of youth years earlier doing what I loved, surrounded by young people who chased extraordinary dreams; I figured he drank from a similar fountain.

I'd heard players describe him as a wizard with *X*'s and *O*'s but also difficult and abrasive. I know that when players say negative things about a coach, it's often a reflection of how much playing time he gives them, so I made no judgments about him until I could spend time with him myself.

He was the new coach of the Bobcats, and I looked forward to meeting him. I'd read that he was Jewish, and since there were so few members of the tribe in the NBA, I hoped I might find an ally. I was standing with a couple of players, and Larry came over and greeted them with man hugs and smiles. I waited for him to extend his hand. He didn't.

I felt like a young boy denied an autograph. Who doesn't shake hands with everyone huddled together in a small group?

It could have been an oversight, but it wouldn't be the first time I'd seen coaches display insecurity when their players trust an outsider to help them develop. In another situation I would have introduced myself, but pro sports are filled with macho personalities who look to assert their dominance in even the most trivial situations, like a handshake. So I trusted my experience and ignored him also, however childish this may seem. Whenever I saw him at the facility, where I was working with Jason Richardson and Ray Felton, we passed each other in the hallway like feuding roommates in a small apartment.

Several weeks later I traveled to Las Vegas to connect with the same players during the NBA's annual summer league. The Bobcats had invited their veterans to optional practices so they could get to know the rookies and new coaching staff. Jason and Ray trained with me in the early mornings and then attended the practices later in the day.

One afternoon, I spotted Larry while I was waiting for Jason and Raymond in the hotel lobby. On impulse, I approached him and extended my hand.

"Hello, Larry, my name is Idan."

He looked at me as if I'd spoken Turkish, and he was probably irritated I didn't call him Coach. Job titles in sports often substituted for first names, to make sure the underlings didn't start thinking they were equals. I know I can be defiant and overthink things, but calling someone by their title just didn't make sense to me. I don't recall hearing anyone referred to as Managing Partner Mike or CEO Sarah or Editor Jeff or Graphic Designer Bobby.

"We're often in the same place around the same people," I continued. "I train many of the players on your roster, so I just wanted to introduce myself and say hello."

"Don't you think you need to ask permission from my assistant coaches before you work with my players?" he asked.

"No, why do I need to ask for their permission?"

The image of him screening my call as if I were a telemarketer flashed across my mind.

"Because these are my players," he said.

"I work with many of the franchise players around the league. Rest assured, your players are in good hands."

"What's a 'franchise player'?" he said sarcastically.

What you were when you played a hundred years ago, I thought, but held my tongue.

"Stars don't need to develop. They are already great," he said.

"They weren't born great." I was getting testy in spite of my best efforts.

"I've coached and been coached by the best," he said, rattling off the names of well-known college and NBA coaches. At that moment I wanted to cover my ears with my hands. "If you want to learn how to develop players, you need to attend my practices."

I walked away.

Religion made me skeptical, law made me indecisive, and

basketball made me rougher. Years ago I would never have argued with someone I'd admired. But the more I saw the inside of the basketball world, the more I recognized that parts of it didn't make sense. I was shocked that a coach would say stars couldn't get better, or that there was nothing a player could learn from anyone but him. That didn't sound like any educator I knew.

Positions in professional sports often resemble political appointments, handed to cronies, old teammates, and friends. You get a job if you're a guy who knows a guy who knows a guy. The hiring decisions often reflect the view that you can only be it if you were of it. I don't agree. There are male gynecologists, female writers who create unforgettable male characters and vice versa, music producers who never played an instrument—and I don't see any reason there can't be great trainers who didn't play college or professional basketball.

I'm certain there are things I could learn from how Larry Brown conducts practices; after all, he represents the Mount Rushmore of basketball coaching. I'm equally sure he could learn some things from watching me. A pretty fair coach named John Wooden once said, "It's what you learn after you know it all that counts."

As for me, my ears and eyes were always open, but I was no longer knocking on doors waiting for a magical opportunity. I didn't have to ask for the job; I was doing it.

II. NO I IN TEAM

if coaches only coached & players only played,
we'd have video games & not sports
#collaborate

The more time I spent around NBA players and teams, the more familiar I became with the league as an institution, and a lot of what I heard from my players and what I saw just didn't make any sense to me.

Communication was mostly a one-way street; coaches and the front office talked, and the players were expected to listen and perform. This was probably the biggest source of frustration for the players. They're excellent and dedicated athletes who've been playing the game all their lives, and they have something more than just their bodies to contribute, but if they try to make suggestions, they get a reputation as "uncoachable" or worse.

Teams expect players to show a kind of humility and loyalty that doesn't come naturally to exceptional performers, and then the teams show no such loyalty in return. They insist that players shelve their personal goals for the best interest of the team, never mentioning the fact that winning keeps the coaches and front office employed. But professional athletes don't relinquish personal goals easily, because they know their contracts, salaries, and bonuses are tied to their individual performance. During contract negotiations, unselfishness and knowing how to win don't go as far as facts and figures do.

They may say there is no *I* in *team*, but money talks louder and shows what's really important to them.

The tension between personal and team goals ripples through most locker rooms—it does through most boardrooms too—and even found its way into my world.

I first met Brendan Haywood, the seven-foot center who played four years at North Carolina, when he was with the Wizards under head coach Eddie Jordan. Brendan and Eddie didn't see eye to eye. According to Brendan, Eddie wanted Brendan to protect the rim and to have a bigger presence in the lane to complement the team's three NBA All-Stars—Gilbert Arenas, Antawn Jamison, and Caron Butler—who preferred to play on the perimeter. Meanwhile, Brendan thought he already did what was expected of him, and attributed any missed assignments, rotations, or rebounds to trying to stay out of early foul trouble.

Reading between the lines, I figured Brendan's concern with early fouls meant he was worried about playing fewer minutes, which would affect his stats, which would impact his agent's leverage during future contract negotiations. If you're in foul trouble all the time, you can't stay on the floor, and if you can't stay on the floor, you can't build up your numbers. It always comes back to money. Always.

Eddie understood this, and he thought Brendan was being selfish. Soon Brendan was expressing his frustrations publicly, and Eddie was cutting his minutes even further. I suspected Brendan thought he was being punished with more bench time for not keeping team issues in-house, and Eddie thought Brendan's public outcry undermined his authority as a head coach. The quickest way to lose the respect of a player is to chop his minutes without an apparent reason; the quickest way for a player to lose the respect of a head coach is to publicly challenge his decisions. It's a story that seems to play out in roughly half the league's locker rooms every single season.

Everything came to a head in a first-round playoff sweep at the hands of the Cleveland Cavaliers, when Eddie sat Brendan for the entire last game. Tempers boiled. Brendan left the bench before the final buzzer; he was gone from the locker room along with the nameplate off his locker by the time the media filed in for comments.

In frustration, Brendan requested a trade directly from the team owner, Abe Pollin. Mr. Pollin summoned his team's GM and insisted Eddie and Brendan find a way to resolve their differences.

That summer Brendan and I were working together in Charlotte, North Carolina. Eddie Jordan was dispatched to Charlotte to try to settle things. Brendan wasn't optimistic, but I encouraged Brendan to hear Eddie, and I let him know that I would mediate if it could help. They needed each other so they could both win games and earn better contracts.

It was a weird position for me, because my own relationship with Eddie was nonexistent. I had trained Brendan, Gilbert Arenas, Juan Dixon, and Steve Blake around that time, using the team's practice facility with its permission. I saw Eddie any number of times, and he never said a single word to me. Nothing. It was probably killing him that so many of his players were coming to me for help, but I certainly didn't want to cause any tension between us, so when I'd see him I'd just nod to him and keep on walking.

Eddie and his lead assistant arrived in Charlotte and came to see Brendan at the Bobcats practice facility. We had just finished our workout, and Brendan was playing pickup with some of the Charlotte guys. Eddie and I found ourselves standing together at the side of the court, and we started talking, and he asked me if I ever had trouble with Brendan.

"Never had trouble with players others would call disruptive or difficult," I answered.

I told him I ask my players for input, and I'm not embarrassed to admit it when there's something I don't know. I consider my relationship with them a partnership where we work on communal goals. This collaboration helps forge a strong relationship, even with players labeled hazardous. Eddie smiled, but I wondered if he thought I was calling him a know-it-all.

"You obviously have an incredible knowledge of the game," I said. "But sometimes, there will be things you don't know or don't know as well. Ask for their input, even if sometimes you don't need it. You'll be surprised with how much they know. Learn from them. I do."

Eddie wasn't sure. He rightfully thought Brendan could be a smart-ass and might challenge him in front of the team. I suggested he keep Brendan more involved. If "team" was the premise of his coaching philosophy, then it should be part of his methodology as well. On the most basic level, this means recognizing that all NBA players can offer valuable insight if you'll let them. Brendan was very bright, but insecurity sometimes triggered his sarcasm. When I spoke to Brendan in the midst of the uproar, he said he didn't intend to undermine authority, but simply wanted to understand why his role was being defined the way it was and why his minutes were reduced. I suggested to Eddie that he ignore the tone of Brendan's questions and just focus on their substance.

Eddie also said he didn't see how he could involve Brendan more when he already had a team with three All-Stars. I said that involvement could mean calling a play for him to start each half, the way the Cleveland Cavaliers had done with Žydrūnas Ilgauskas, and wasn't necessarily confined to the court. Eddie could invite Brendan to his office to discuss strategy, request his input during film sessions, encourage him to mentor the rookies, and even amplify the coaching staff's messages.

"You think he's challenging you, but all you have to do is ask his opinion," I told him. "Brendan's a cerebral guy. Empower him."

Eddie nodded, but he was worried that giving Brendan a forum would mean he'd have to extend that courtesy to all his players.

"Precisely," I answered.

I hoped Eddie would seek the collective input of his players, and Brendan would acknowledge his mistakes. To be honest, though, I wasn't really sure that Eddie was paying much attention to what I was saying.

The next week the newspapers reported that Eddie visited Brendan in Charlotte to resolve their differences. Eddie was quoted as saying a number of things that were surprisingly similar to the advice I shared with him. That was extremely encouraging and gratifying.

There is no *I* in *team*, but there are two in *listening*.

III. THROWN TO THE 'WOLVES

*it looks easy because it took a lifetime 2 perfect
#practice*

Ties were loosened, sleeves were rolled, and oversized suit jackets with multiple buttons—the remains from playing careers in the '80s and '90s—hung on the backs of chairs as the Minnesota Timberwolves coaching staff discussed their most recent loss. I didn't want to be there, but David Kahn, the GM, had insisted I join the meeting.

Once upon a time, this would have been my dream—to sit in with the coaches of an NBA team, any NBA team, as they went about their postgame analysis, to participate in the process of making its players better. I had sent out résumés, followed up with phone calls, and pursued all avenues for the chance to contribute in any way. Not so many years ago, I would have been happy to diagram an opponent's plays, break down video, Xerox game plans, and stick them in binders—whatever a team wanted me to do.

But I was no longer so eager to find my way inside the fortress. I preferred working directly with the players in an atmosphere of trust, where each of them knew I had his interests at heart. There were no divided loyalties this way, no questions about whether I was doing what's best for the player.

I had agreed to come and spend some time with the Timberwolves as an experiment; I was curious to see if an organization would let me do my thing on a consulting basis, with freedom and autonomy to work no differently from if I were working with the players on my own. I was skeptical. I knew that Larry Brown and Eddie Jordan were hardly the only coaches who felt proprietary about their players and were quick to see criticism behind every idea that came from someone else.

David Kahn had assured me that I could set things up the

way I wanted without the staff imposing any conditions. That sounded good but unlikely. Perched at the head of the table, David introduced me by explaining the purpose of my visit. I was excited to work with the team for the week, but I sensed the coaching staff's unease, as if my presence suggested their work product was subpar. That was never my intention, only to help where I could.

Kurt Rambis was the head coach; I had always enjoyed watching him play on national television when I was young, because his tough style of play was a perfect complement to the "Showtime" Lakers. Kurt asked for my assessment of his team's play that evening. It was premature for me to comment, I explained, since this was the first time I'd seen the team play up close. "You won't hurt my feelings," he said. I was sure I would have, so again I respectfully declined.

I should probably mention that the Timberwolves were 14–49 at that point and had just lost by fourteen at home to a mediocre Houston team.

He asked about my plans for his players. When I originally spoke with David several days earlier, I agreed I would work with two groups of three players, for two one-hour sessions before practice. The players would then have more than an hour to recover before the start of practice. I thought that would address any concerns he had about working the players too hard too close to practice. Nope: He said he considered the rest period too *long*. I was an outsider, so he was determined to find something wrong with whatever I suggested. I recommended they maximize their time by meeting with their strength coach and athletic trainers, eating breakfast, watching film, and preparing for practice. He repeated that he didn't want his players to sit idly. Neither did I, so I again said his players could make use of the time.

He insisted his staff observe each workout. I agreed to open the sessions to him and David if that would ease their concerns;

the sessions would be closed to his assistants. He didn't understand how I could take this stance, coming to his facility to work with his players yet dictating who could attend. I wondered privately if he threw a similar tantrum when his players met with physicians, psychologists, and physical therapists. I reminded David that we'd agreed beforehand that the workouts would be closed.

"I prefer closed gyms because they create a better learning environment," I told the room. "Players become transparent. They can make mistakes, work on their weaknesses, and talk candidly with someone who doesn't control their minutes or their paychecks. There is no judgment and I don't report back to anyone. What happens in the gym stays in the gym."

Neither Kurt nor his staff nodded their heads, or moved their arms, or kicked their feet in the air, or did anything to acknowledge I'd even spoken. They sat expressionless, as if channel surfing on the couch in the late evening after eating an extra-large pizza.

After a few seconds of silence from everyone including David, Kurt tried to argue that his staff needed to be there to reinforce proper mechanics.

If they had proper mechanics, I wouldn't be here, I thought.

He also worried that I would overwork his players before practice. "Why would I run them into the ground?" I responded.

The open sessions would compromise player privacy and the effectiveness of our efforts. I had worked too hard to retreat because the establishment didn't agree with my position.

As if waving the white flag, Kurt pulled on his tie until it hung loosely from his collar, and then pushed a pen across the table. I guess he wanted me to take notes. He identified every player's deficiencies. I had never agreed to work with the entire team. I pretended to scribble some notes while they rambled.

I arrived at the facility early the next morning to meet with the first group of guards: Jonny Flynn, Corey Brewer, and Ramon Sessions. They shuffled their feet as they approached the practice court. Their strides were heavy and short, and they spent more time tying the drawstrings on their shorts than they did warming up. I'm sure they wondered how several days of additional morning training late in the season could benefit any of them.

This group included first-round draft picks with stellar college careers who thus far in their young careers had suffered injuries and played in systems not geared to their strengths and for teams that needed their young players to excel immediately. In professional sports, coaches and front office personnel can lose their jobs when highly touted players underperform, because it reflects badly on their ability to forecast performance and develop talent. Teams often lose patience quickly and devalue their players even quicker. Young players have to confront the uncertainty created when their team's perception of their abilities differs from their own. This takes its toll on their love of the game.

To the athletes, I hoped I represented a fresh voice, energy, optimism, perspective, and philosophy, conveyed by someone who didn't need to be there other than because I believed in them. I intended to remind them that the game required a child's love and attention, while also challenging them with intense, creative, and functional drills. I hoped they would reconnect with that joy and again create magic on the court.

With David and Kurt observing from the sidelines, there was an awkward energy in the gym before we started, the coach uneasy about letting someone new instruct his players and the GM questioning the wisdom of bringing me in in the first place. For the next fifty-five minutes, I belted out directions: "stay small," "more speed," and "torso up, not forward." You would have thought a DJ had hijacked the gym from the sounds of sneaker soles performing like turntables as they scratched the floor, the staccato beat and bass vibrating as the ball pounded the court, and the clatter from hands slapping together like cymbals as teammates supported one another. The athletes repeatedly looked in my direction, searching for feedback. Afterward, they asked for our schedule for the remaining days. Their desire for self-improvement had replaced the feelings of distrust and apathy I'd sensed earlier.

Kurt alerted me that our session had lasted nearly an hour. The night before he'd expressed concern that I would overwork his players, so I took that to heart. I reminded him that three players had trained together for only fifty-five minutes, with at least a ninety-second rest interval between sets.

There was a similar lethargy in the second group, consisting of front-court players: Kevin Love, Darko Miličić, and Sasha Pavlović. I could see Kevin was destined for greatness; there was a precision and economy to his movements, and he was interested in every detail. He was something of a scientist in his approach; pro basketball is a world of imprecise athletes who overcome their deficiencies with otherworldly talent, but Kevin recognizes that he can compensate for what he may lack in athleticism with diligence and skill.

I found myself worrying about Darko, a player labeled hazardous because he had never lived up to expectations. He was the second pick in the 2003 draft, taken after LeBron James and before Carmelo Anthony, Chris Bosh, and Dwyane Wade. When an athlete perceives himself as a potential star, he can have trouble adjusting to a lesser role and struggle to succeed in his limited opportunities. Darko seemed scarred and timid, probably from all the years of criticism. He reminded me of a puppy one of my players adopted who'd been left homeless after Hurricane Katrina; it cowered when it heard loud noise, retreated to the laundry room when it saw an unfamiliar face, quivered at the sight of an extended hand, and even scurried from the kitchen when its owner poured food into its bowl.

Seven years into his pro career and only twenty-four, Darko still needed a team to be patient and overlook his mistakes on the court, or he would never become the player he could be, or even the player he once was: a teenager with dreams of stardom.

The session started with conditioning and back-to-basket drills that centered on footwork and scoring. Darko jogged rather than ran. He kidded with teammates rather than focus on his technique. He retrieved the ball with his feet, dribbling it like a soccer ball. Maybe I'd been too quick to defend him; perhaps the root of his past problems wasn't his critics but rather not enough accountability. I changed tactics quickly.

"You aren't that good yet to be screwing around," I said to him as he ran past me.

The arrow struck his pride, and he responded to the small dose of honesty. He soon impressed me with his mobility, his high release, and how effortlessly he exploded from the floor. I applauded his effort and smacked his hand when he ran by.

"You have so much ability, but you hide it," I said.

The next day I saw one of the assistant coaches at Starbucks. He said he didn't understand my rationale for closed training sessions, and he thought I was making too big a deal about it.

"It's just basketball, man. This ain't rocket science," he said.

He didn't get it. They never got it. If replicating what they saw was all it took, then anyone could have guided the Los Angeles Lakers to multiple NBA titles while running the triangle offense. But there's so much more to it. Phil Jackson had something special. He helped his players feel something special, and his players responded by doing something special.

I want the players I'm working with to feel something special too. Call it inspiration, drive, joy, or simply connection: It's the reason I've been able to carve out a place for myself in the game I love. It's why I've never wavered in my convictions while challenging the culture and protocol of the institution; why I can burrow into the lives of the most famous athletes in the world and earn their complete trust; why they respond to my texts and phone calls; why we train hard, efficiently, and with focus in the early mornings despite the long evenings prior; why I teach them to become comfortable with the uncomfortable; why I must win their faith, so they'll digest my lessons and implement them when they play and hear my words despite the distractions all around them; why I try so hard to restore their enthusiasm for the game; why they improve on and off the court; and why they compensate me even though they receive almost everything else in the world for free.

Nothing much changed for the Timberwolves after my week with them. There was too much institutional resistance for the players and me to take more than baby steps. I still see the players in my travels, and we chat and shoot the shit like we'd developed a bit of a bond.

I don't see much of Kurt Rambis or that assistant I ran into in Starbucks.

If it's not rocket science, it's because it's a lot harder and more important than that.

It's love.

CHAPTER THIRTY

FIFTEEN MINUTES

every level of success brings another layer of hard
#lifeaintnevereasy

My memories of law school are few and vague. Thousands of hours in the law library and in the same classrooms blend together to form an overcast sky with an occasional hailstorm of recalled distress.

One of the few moments that ring with specificity came in a sports law class, when the professor assigned us to identify a sports-related dispute and analyze the issues in the context of topics in our syllabus. I hazily recalled an article by a senior writer at *Sports Illustrated* detailing an investigation of a basketball coach and his university. I wasn't sure the subject matter of the investigation amounted to the kind of dispute the assignment required, but I was in my third year of law school and I didn't give a shit. It involved basketball, and I could mold it to work for me.

I couldn't find any material in the legal database LexisNexis, so I hoped the senior writer at *SI* would share with me some of his research before I outlined the assignment. A receptionist at *SI* transferred me to his voice mail. Late one evening, I returned home after class to find the message light blinking on my answering machine. "Holy shit!" Someone from the magazine I had worshipped as a teenager actually returned my call.

My parents knew little about sports and didn't actively support it, but for some reason they permitted me to order the weekly sports magazine. I would thumb through *SI* while lying on my belly until bedtime, ignoring how the imprint from the thinly carpeted floors of our family basement was becoming painfully embedded in my elbows and knees. *SI* became my bible, photo album, textbook, and diary. I read every word, studied every photo, and memorized every anecdote. I stacked the magazines chronologically, making sure not to crease any of the pages, and would then reread them with the same original excitement. I daydreamed while reviewing the long-running *SI* segment Faces in the Crowd, which featured amateur athletes who set milestones. I prayed one day *SI* would feature my profile and basketball accomplishments. I gently touched the pages, hoping it would bring me closer to the athletes and the game.

The writer, Alexander Wolff, and I eventually spoke. He mailed me whatever documents he thought could help. My professor issued me a C on an assignment I considered well done. "The subject matter you selected didn't amount to a legal dispute," he explained. I tried to care, but I cared more about the game than I did about the breach of contract, antitrust, and monopoly issues that excited him and my classmates.

Ten years later, I received a call from another senior writer at *SI*. This time, though, Chris Ballard wanted to meet as part of his research for a book he intended to write about pro ball. Over dinner I cautiously explained my love affair with the game, my philosophies, my observations, my perceptions of the athletes I trained, and my thoughts on dealing with the basketball institution. A devoted father, husband, writer, and fan, Chris struck me as a good guy and passionate about the game, but I didn't trust easily, especially in the context of the institution of sports. I shared with him only enough to help him tell his story.

Months later I learned that the information he gained from our conversations would appear as a chapter in his book *The Art of a Beautiful Game.* This child from a religious immigrant family who never played the game past high school would now share the spotlight with the future Hall of Famers he admired. Chris dedicated a chapter to Dwight Howard and shot blocking, to Steve Kerr and the mentality of a pure shooter, to LeBron James and his physical gifts, and even revealed the roots of Kobe Bryant's killer instinct. And alongside those would be a chapter devoted to understanding how I burrow my way into the minds of the athletes I train.

I was just a regular guy with irregular dreams. I never thought someone would find me or my journey interesting. This couldn't be happening.

And it continued. The October 26, 2009, edition of *SI* featured the chapter Chris devoted to me in its NBA preview edition. Even the cover referenced me: THE HOOPS WHISPERER appeared in white capital letters above the photo of Shaq and LeBron on the front above the logo. After buying multiple copies of the magazine, I stared at the pages, recalling how I'd pleaded to the heavens since childhood for an extraordinary life. My life has been filled with these if-they-only-knew moments. If they only knew the strength of my faith and my daydreams; my heartfelt appreciation that they considered my story inspiring; my humility knowing where it all began; my exasperation with loving something without a destination; my longing for acknowledgment after decades of anonymity behind closed gym doors; the unlikelihood of a national print publication running a seven-page feature about someone whose name meant nothing to the public, without a publicist, mentor, manager, or agent zealously advocating on behalf of the protagonist.

My life changed after the feature ran. I became more visible and vulnerable, gaining fans and critics. Some found me inspiring, while others thought I sold magic beans. Some felt liberated to do what they loved, while others thought formal education and experience were prerequisites. Some considered my work genius, while others thought they could easily replicate my efforts. I hoped the seesaw of support and criticism would fade, but it hasn't.

Several days later, NBA TV, as part of its regular season preview, interviewed me along with another trainer. He spoke first, introducing himself with his education, degrees, and playing experience. Too coincidental, I thought. I anticipated his subtle jabs but declined to throw back. I briefly summarized who I was and what I did, and I thanked my would-be adversary for helping Gilbert Arenas with his knee rehab during the off-season. The teeter-totter soon rocketed upward.

While I was in Phoenix working with some of the Suns players, Steve Kerr, the team's GM at the time, surprisingly greeted me with open arms and thanked me for making time for his guys. Ironically, the range and frequency of opinions helped me better empathize with my athletes. I tell them we'll never discuss public opinion, because that noise affects the blood pressure.

I wish could say I always took my own advice, but I couldn't completely muffle the chatter. I also felt pressure to create magic. Suddenly everyone wanted to know my secret, as if I could demonstrate it on command or transform it into fifteen minutes of motivational bullets that would change lives forever. I even fielded calls from television agents and prominent production companies who hoped to capture this magic on camera. But despite their expectations and financial incentives, I don't have a formula or pill to make people amazing. My work involves gradual self-improvement, spiritual transformation and empowerment, joy, reconnecting with childhood, and living by faith, not by dreams; it takes a lifetime to absorb and it doesn't translate into sixty minutes of weekly television.

Even though I knew better, this scrutiny and pressure to deliver immediate greatness caused me stress, put me on the defensive with my critics, forced me into deeper seclusion with my athletes when we trained, and left me with a new appreciation for everything they face. Each game requires them to carry their franchise, city, and community on their shoulders. The audience marvels at the obviously amazing plays but doesn't recognize the greatness required to make the game look easy. Every open shot by Melo or CP seems simple, but it represents a mastery of mechanics, movement, thought, and confidence; thousands of shots taken at the same distance and angle; and, most important, a culmination of decisions made over a lifetime that brought them to this moment. I often wondered if an athlete sometimes elevates the degree of difficulty in a play simply to demonstrate his greatness and the futility of trying to replicate it.

In the wake of my fifteen minutes of fame I faced a similar pressure to deliver instant magic to show the world that not everyone who'd ever played and loved the game could do what I do. A bounce of a ball, a pass, drill, sprint, direction, leap, hurdle, shot, and bound certainly looks simple; the complexity comes from the context, movement, application, intensity, and intuition created to echo those of a performance. To walk along a two-by-four is easy; to walk along one propped between two forty-story buildings takes specialized training in absolute focus. I never anticipated I would have to confront the pressure of recognition, and hoped I could one day tune out the skeptics and the fans as well as my players did.

My guys were right. Every level of success does bring another level of hard.

CHAPTER THIRTY-ONE

BRAND AMBASSADOR

God gives us the ingredients not the recipe
#menu

Michael Jordan, the founder and chairman of Jordan Brand, represented everything I had wanted to be when I was a child. I worshipped his game, memorized his stats, bought his posters with whatever money my grandma gifted me, pleaded with my parents to buy me a pair of his signature shoes, wore a sweatband on my forearm and a black kneepad when I played just because he did, and impersonated his dunks on the nine-foot rims in the neighborhood. More important, if he couldn't make varsity as a high school sophomore, maybe persistence, passion, and determination could also bring me a wonderful life, even if I didn't know at the age of fourteen what that life could entail.

So when a few folks over at Nike's Jordan Brand asked if I wanted to spearhead the program's training component, I answered, "Yeah!" in half an instant. The Jordan Brand Flight Ambassador program is a convergence of community outreach and product launch. While drawing attention to the company's wares, the program provides sound basketball instruction to any kids who come to its free clinics. There were hundreds of them in a Manhattan gym one day, spread around two full courts, and I was there in my uniform—a newly minted matching sweat suit and sneakers—to lead a clinic as a representative of Michael Jordan's namesake brand.

With the help of my team of Flight Ambassadors, I divided roughly two hundred participants into twenty rows of ten and positioned them along each sideline.

"Get into a squat position, thrust your arms back, then jump forward as far as you can," I commanded. "Both feet should strike the ground at the same time while you stabilize your landing. Avoid the wiggle."

The pool of young players varied in age, size, skill level, and experience. I noticed who jumped the farthest, landed the softest, stood the tallest, adapted the quickest, asked relevant questions, ignored their peers and the hip-hop spun by the DJ in the corner, skipped line for another try, and even practiced on the side until it was their turn.

"Learn to put the brakes on the Ferrari," I urged as I watched the more advanced players maintain a four-count pace of a one-second jump, one-second land, and two-second pause.

To demonstrate the physicality of pro ball, I had them stand in a defensive posture, then I pressed hard with the heel of my hand against their front shoulders and tapped their sternums with my palm to drive them backward, even tugged on their arms to draw them off-balance. This was something television and video games can't truly convey. I wondered whether this aggressive interaction was too intense for the parents watching from the sideline, but I wanted my young audience to feel the correlation between strength, balance, and contact.

And then I focused on the others. There were some players in attendance that morning who ignored precision, gave limited effort, feared embarrassment, joked with their peers, and cared more about free product than free instruction. The program wasn't designed as a clinic for the city's best players, and a deep love of the game wasn't a prerequisite. Yet I couldn't help comparing the young audience with myself at that age. I would have been so eager as a teenager to attend a basketball clinic fronted by a global brand and offering great instruction and access to a basketball-loving community. But not everyone at this session felt the same, and this explained their lack of focus, intensity, and awareness. I wondered if their ambivalence reflected my inability to engage them, or if they were only there to satisfy the vicarious wishes of overzealous parents.

While I surveyed the stations at each basket designated for shooting, passing, and competitive games, some parents introduced themselves to me.

"Which one is yours?" I asked.

"The one wearing ———," they would answer, while also summarizing their child's work ethic and accomplishments to date. It seemed as though every parent described their child as a tireless worker and destined to play major-college ball.

"Would it be possible for you to work with my child?" they asked.

I paused.

"I'm sorry, I can't."

Some thought their children could become stars with a little fine-tuning, while others were surprised by my honesty. Plenty of trainers target young people, but I prefer to go in a different direction.

"Figure out first if they love the game," I said.

This meant trusting their children to lead, and even limiting the availability of resources. Would the kids still play ball if there were no organized practices, reserved gyms, trainers, trendy sneakers and gear, health clubs, and coaches? I did, and it became my internal proof of how much the game meant to me, as well as the source of my self-reliance, resourcefulness, and discipline.

"Of course they love the game," the parents answered without hesitation.

"Would your child really pocket their allowance to save for a rope to skip at home if the trainer wasn't available? Would they bound the basement stairs if you canceled the gym membership? Would they run sprints on the coldest days at the park if they didn't have practice at school? Would they shovel snow to clear a path along the driveway to work on their handle if you wouldn't drive them to the gym?"

I didn't wait for their answers and excused myself before returning to the court. I hoped the parents would convey those rhetorical questions to their children and that the kids would give them some serious thought.

I continued to patrol the gym, offering instruction and encouragement where I could, my voice amplified by the microphone handed to me earlier by the DJ. I tended to speak quickly and to not edit my thoughts, but I was careful at that moment not to turn the microphone into a flamethrower. For most teenagers, self-esteem and peer acceptance are interconnected. Broadcasting their mistakes could embarrass them and, more important, dissuade them from experimenting by creating an association between errors and shame. When I could, I muted the microphone and spoke to individuals with a firm but supportive tone.

"I'd rather you miss the right way than make the wrong way," I said to a few of them. Some understood my message and became more deliberate with their technique. A few made no changes. To those who weren't giving the effort I hoped, I shared with them that Melo's smile and CP's lightheartedness masked a ferocious level of commitment. To those more concerned with their matching outfits, I pointed out that Beats by Dre headphones, fly clothes, and diamond earrings don't make someone a pro ballplayer. To those reluctant to try, I said that some of the greatest players in the world retreat into their lairs every off-season and, with amazing dedication and focus, labor in private to reinvent themselves in preparation for the new campaign.

The comments still didn't make a difference for some of them. The game wasn't that important to them at that moment, perhaps at all. I was disappointed, but it wasn't my place to make demands; training wasn't about fulfilling my wants but rather magnifying theirs. Maybe they had already made choices reflecting their interests and gifts without realizing it. Perhaps those whose priority was the matching outfits and trendy sneakers were meant for a creative career in design or fashion. Maybe the ones inclined to chat with friends on the sidelines were meant for a career in sales. And perhaps those reluctant to try were inclined to observe and document, with a future in media, journalism, or publishing.

The goal of the program isn't to create pro ballplayers. For me, its intention is to socialize its young audience to the process of success. I hoped our session would show that effort, awareness, persistence, diligence, commitment, passion, and faith are necessary in chasing what really matters to you. In fairness to the kids attending, many didn't know yet what that might be. I hoped they would have the courage and patience to try to discover the answer, and then to experience all the unexpected happiness and necessary sadness that comes with the pursuit of something you love.

When asked to help create the framework for the program many months earlier, I'd thought of four words that seemed to embody its purpose.

"Flight Ambassadors: Where Dreams Take Flight," I had written in an e-mail to a colleague.

I was genuinely shocked when the marketing team decided to use my suggestion, but the words certainly described our intentions. I can't think of a worthier goal than to help others achieve their dreams.

CHAPTER THIRTY-TWO

THE WORK, NOT THE JOB

roses may be red, violets not always blue,
reason I know, I chose a life with a different hue
#theroadnottaken

I arrived early to the small college campus in downtown Chicago for another Flight Ambassador program event, coinciding with the release of Chris Paul's signature shoe. I recognized most of the faces except for Lisa, a young woman in her early twenties standing at half-court, dressed in matching Nike Jordan Brand tee, shorts, and sneakers. I assumed she was local and had volunteered to assist with today's event. I said hello and introduced myself. She did the same and inquired about my role.

After I explained, she asked some more questions about my background and playing experience. She seemed perplexed as to how I'd earned this gig since I didn't have the same formal organized basketball résumé as she. I anticipated an unrelenting curiosity, born from the sentiment of *Why him, not me?* so I channeled the conversation toward her. As I expected, she'd played college ball and aspired to coach in college. She attended coaching clinics and networked with high-profile coaches and sports personalities.

I could tell where she was heading because she littered her conversation with bread crumbs. I wondered why she thought developing relationships with the institution and mimicking what she saw would make her better at her craft and open doors.

I finally interrupted her to say, "You've become too institutionalized."

She looked puzzled and irritated, as if she'd been punched in the belly and wanted to retaliate. She held her tongue, the way we do when we hear something dismissive from a person in authority.

Talking with her brought to mind the countless résumés and e-mails I receive begging for an opportunity to help develop and train pro athletes.

In some ways, she even reminded me of me.

But I have a natural predisposition not to blend with the institution—any institution. It was something I first discovered at an early age during homeroom roll call at a public elementary school I attended. I soon recognized that not only did my name make me unusual, but so did my experience and perspective. An immigrant family fighting to preserve its traditions, my parents had an us-versus-them philosophy. Their thick accents, unusual first names, religious observance, Israeli military service, reluctance to adopt American cultural signifiers no matter how playful and secular, choice of profession, and insistence on tradition reflected a profound unwillingness to assimilate. Their defiance had its consequences, alienating those whose priorities were to conform and to not make waves. My father had to move thousands of miles away from his family to find employment because our local Jewish community chose not to hire him for any teaching or administrative position in Judaic Studies. The tension I sensed between my family and the Jewish community was similar to that of families who traveled from Africa to the United States and didn't embrace African-American culture quickly enough.

I learned defiance and nonconformity through osmosis, yet like every child I wanted to fit in because the other side always looked so bright. I pleaded to attend public school, spend weekend afternoons at the mall, attend overnight summer camp, trick-or-treat, and host or attend sleepovers. No, my parents said. When my love for the game became so intense during middle and high school, that desire to belong transitioned to the basketball community. I wanted to attend the best basketball schools, play against the best players, and garner the attention of the college programs. No, my parents said.

When I left for college, I leaped onto the largest stage to audition before a basketball community that I knew too little about. I was good, but not good enough yet to devise my own set of rules and batter my way in. I had to rely on that community to appreciate my subtle gifts. They didn't.

Years later, when I was pursuing a life change, I swung my arms and bounded as high as I could, like a shipwrecked man who had just seen the rescue plane from the desert island. I wanted the basketball community to rescue me from my plight. The résumés, handshakes, phone calls, e-mails, informational meetings, and assorted efforts represented my SOS. I prayed for the chance to become part of a locker room again, to feel camaraderie, to share in victory and defeat, to spend time on a court with the game's best, to experience what I loved every day, and to finally feel comfortable in a community that understood how much an orange leather ball can really mean.

No, they said.

The NBA represented the big house at the end of the cul-de-sac where the popular neighborhood kids played after school, where the best snacks were served, and where they threw the most lavish birthday parties. It stood for everything I thought I wanted, but the invitation never came. I finally couldn't wait any longer for a chance, so I hosted my own parties, however small they were. Amazingly enough, word spread about those quiet little parties, and eventually some of the popular kids were knocking at my door and asking if they could come in. The folks in the shiny palace noticed, and they opened their doors and gave me a peek inside.

While I was still at the stage of networking and trying to find my way into the institution, a mutual friend offered to connect me with Donnie Nelson, the general manager of the Dallas Mavericks at the time. He described Donnie as progressive, someone with a great eye for talent regardless of its shape, size, or origin.

I thought, *After all my efforts, here's my chance to show them what I can do.*

Donnie and I spoke briefly and made arrangements to meet in the lobby of the team hotel when the Mavericks played the Wizards in Washington.

"Call my room when you get here," he instructed.

I arrived at the Four Seasons Hotel dressed in a suit and tie. I dialed the house phone to connect me to the room of "Donnie Nelson."

"Wrong number," Don Nelson Sr., the head coach at the time, said when he answered.

I dialed again, and this time I reluctantly left a voice mail, concerned that the message forfeited my right to call again. I waited in the lobby, gripping my cell tightly so I could feel it vibrate. It didn't. I debated whether to leave. Stalking and persistence were close cousins and depended on the perspective of the audience. I didn't know Donnie well, but when I saw him enter the foyer I charged toward him as he approached the elevators.

"Donnie!" I called out.

I introduced myself because we had never met in person. I reminded him of our meeting.

"Idaaaaaan, good to finally meet you! Let me drop off my things in my room and I will be down in a few."

Once he returned I formally summarized my work with NBA players, my background in law, my passion, and my interest in exploring full-time opportunities with an NBA team. He prefaced his answer with an overview of his hiring practices. He preferred to hire people he "had been in the trenches with." I instantly imagined all the former players he had hired; also the draft picks and free agents he signed over the years with whom he'd never shared a foxhole and who were represented by agents he disliked. Donnie himself had broken into basketball the old-fashioned way: by being the son of Hall of Fame coach Don Nelson, who hired him as a scout and later an assistant.

He had no full-time positions available, he said, but to my surprise he suggested I visit Dallas for a few days because he had some work for me to do.

Music to my ears, even though I didn't know the song, hook, vocals, or instrumentals. I hoped it would include a scouting project—or, even better, time on the court with one of his players.

I purchased a round-trip ticket to Dallas and reserved a hotel room within walking distance of Donnie's office, the American-Airlines Arena. When I landed at Dallas/Fort Worth Airport, JC, a scout from the Mavericks' front office, met me curbside and gave me a lift to my hotel.

"No idea," JC said with a laugh when I inquired about the project for which Donnie wanted my assistance.

JC escorted me to the arena later in the day so I could meet with Donnie. I waited for him in a conference room along with his other guests, coaches from overseas professional leagues. Donnie greeted everyone. I don't remember the precise conversation, but I do recall the expressions of awe and gratitude from the foreigners, excited to have touched NBA life.

Maybe he'll assign my project later, I thought.

I was back at the arena the next day, again anticipating my assignment. Donnie escorted me and a few of the international coaches to the practice court. We stood along the catwalk overlooking the court and adjacent to Donnie's office, where guests and team personnel watch practice. I recognized two former NBA players who were now Mavericks assistant coaches. Donnie suggested I introduce myself to them.

"What a great way for you to experience the NBA," one of the assistants said.

Donnie leaned over the catwalk railing to toss me a pair of grossly oversized basketball sneakers. Apparently he didn't want me to scuff the floor with my hard-bottom shoes. *Random toss, random shoes*, I thought.

Donnie later invited me and the international coaches to the Mavericks' corporate apartment. While there, he circled the room asking each coach for their best in-bounds play. Strange, I thought. Since I'd arrived I had become increasingly skeptical of the motivations behind my invitation to Dallas. I wondered why these coaches would barter strategy for the "NBA experience."

Skepticism soon turned to annoyance. I had come to assist on a project, not to go on a field trip. Again I approached Donnie to ask about the assignment. He looked surprised, as if he had never made that pledge. Eventually he wavered, saying he would try to arrange some time for me to work with one of the Mavericks' nonrotation players, Jon Stefansson.

I arrived at the arena early the following morning ready to work with Jon. The session began with a series of layups performed with the ball extended high and away from his body. Donnie soon interrupted. He asked where I had learned that drill.

Strange question, I thought. "In my head," I answered.

Donnie ended the session within thirty minutes.

"That was very good," he said. "We should have you down here another time to work with a few more of our guys."

I was so excited. On one of my last days in Dallas he invited me and the international coaches to lunch at Hooters. We ate, they talked ball, I listened. When the bill arrived, Donnie handed a Hooters coupon to the waitress.

"Fifty percent off," he said happily.

He then told us how much our share of the bill came to. Each guest at the table paid for his own meal. My skepticism grew.

Weeks later, the Mavericks had an extended home stay and I followed up with Donnie about our last conversation in Dallas. He suggested I come back to work with some of their rookies. I made my own travel arrangements, once again paying for my flight. Donnie wanted me to work with rookies Josh Howard, Jon Stefansson, and Marquis Daniels before practice and games. I overheard him remind his two assistant coaches in charge of player development to watch and absorb whatever they could from me. At that moment in my life, I considered that flattery; today, it seems more like theft.

For the next few days I worked with Josh, Jon, and Marquis. I thought it made sense to have extra training sessions for players who don't play consistent minutes in the rotation. I assumed that I would spend some time with them on the practice court before games, but the players asked me to meet them on the main floor. It was the first time I ever set foot on an NBA court. I hid my enthusiasm and inexperience, because I figured that revealing my excitement would mark me as an impostor in a macho industry like pro sports. But I felt transported in time, back to the University of Maryland and walk-on tryouts: the floor had the precise amount of give, the basketballs were perfectly inflated; the backboards were wiped clean to eliminate any hand and ball prints, and the thousands of empty seats seemed to drift endlessly beyond my horizon. My heart raced in anticipation, and I felt proud because I knew where this had all began.

After we finished our first session on the main floor, I asked the equipment manager to issue me a couple of pairs of practice shorts and tops with the Mavericks logo. This uniform would keep arena security from constantly asking for my on-court credentials, but, more important, would provide the validation I assumed the veteran players would need before I approached them about working with them. I figured Donnie was far too busy even to take note of what I was doing prior to the start of a game, and it's always easier to ask forgiveness than to get permission.

Before I could reach that point, however, the team went on an extended West Coast road trip and it was time for me to head home. Donnie requested I stay a few additional days to work with Jon because he wasn't going west with the team.

"I want him to be your priority when we are gone," Donnie said.

I agreed.

In all, I was in Dallas for about eight or nine days. I came at the team's invitation and did the work they asked me to do. I was never paid for it, never reimbursed for my flights or hotel rooms, and it never led to anything more substantial. At the same time, I didn't tell them the price for my services, or even send them a lengthy invoice for all my expenses. I looked at it as my institutional internship.

In hindsight I appreciate the opportunity, and the Mavericks did me a favor. I was desperate for a chance and unknowingly relinquished my power to Donnie and the institution when I told him of my dissatisfaction with the law and my dreams of full-time NBA employment. I didn't realize yet that disclosing your dreams to savvy people meant they could hold them close enough for you to see but too far away for you to touch. Donnie was a good man—hardworking, friendly—and I generally enjoyed his company and conversation. He did what was best for him and his team, and I respect him for that. Part of what was best for him was to let me think it was best for me to remain in Dallas and work with Jon Stefansson because I was so eager to please.

I had gained an invaluable look inside the gilded doors, though I was disappointed I had let the experience bring back my eager insecurities. I knew my efforts had value, and there was no need for me to give them away. I had something to contribute, and I was doing so with the players who found their way to me. If I were ever to work within a team in the future, it would have to be on a very different basis, with a progressive and open-minded organization that values the unconventional and recognizes the equity I bring to the relationship because of my expertise and track record.

I kept doing what I love: working with amazing people who have otherworldly talent, accepting my own natural gift for understanding their needs and communicating with them to help them hone their skills to the sharpest edge.

And now here I was in Chicago, leading the players and instructors in the Flight Ambassador program, taking note of how Lisa interacted with her players. I didn't micromanage or offer direction. I wanted to see what she would do on her own with limited guidance.

At the end of the ninety-minute session, many of the young campers in attendance thanked the Flight Ambassadors. One of the teenage girls hugged Lisa.

It was time for me to go, but first I sought out Lisa for a final word. I knew why she thought the key to the institution lay in following its ways, and she had hoped to learn something about how I'd forged my path. But the only thing anyone can learn from my journey is that they'll have to make their own.

"You have it," I told her. "That girl hugged you because she can feel and see how much you care. Stop convincing people and just be you. You have *it*. Someone will take notice."

The institution is like a beautiful woman who won't notice you until you decide to ignore her. Lisa wanted someone to give her a chance, to discover her, to validate her gifts. But she had everything she needed to chase her passions. She coaches high school ball and has access to loads of teenage girls who play. If she is as good as she thinks, she has a chance to leave her fingerprints on their lives while doing what she loves. Before her lies the opportunity to produce a legion of Division I and even WNBA players. What more could she want?

Lisa couldn't see that opportunity quite yet. I hoped she eventually would. I hoped she would tinker with her dream and reframe her conventional approach. I hoped she wouldn't wait for the gun to fire before she began the race. I hoped she would ignore the institution, build her own programs, and, from time to time, even toss rocks at the beautiful palace walls.

It takes faith and love. But what that's worthwhile doesn't?

"You think my ex misses me? You think she will ever come back into my life?" one of the players asked me.

"Only when you are happy and in a new relationship," I answered.

"Really?"

"They always miss you when you no longer miss them."

CHAPTER THIRTY-THREE

OUT OF THE SHADOWS

we 4give a child who is afraid of the dark;
the tragedy is when men r afraid of the light
#platonic

When I stand alone on a court with Melo or CP or JR or KD or Steph or, for that matter, any of my guys, I know how fortunate I am. I was lucky to learn my craft on my own, to develop my methods without anyone looking over my shoulder, to earn the trust of superstars based solely on how we worked together, respected each other, communicated, and improved something we both hold sacred. Had my early pleas to be anointed by the institution or even chosen for a job with some team—any team—been answered, I wonder whether I could have conjured up this magical life.

I had the wonderful freedom to figure things out, to improvise, to test ideas, to try new things without wondering if they'd look silly to someone viewing from the outside. The same thing I recognize in my guys is true for me: To learn means you have to be willing to try and to fail without concern for the consequences, until the new becomes the familiar and patterns are ingrained—at which point you start again, creating new variables to allow for new adaptations.

Would a team have approved a drill in which I toss tennis balls to a dribbler to help develop his capacity to deal with distraction? I don't know, and I didn't need to know. The word *approved* had no meaning for me and my guys.

I'm fortunate that I've had a great deal of life experience that has nothing to do with basketball. The game has always been a source of fascination and joy to me, a huge part of my life, but it's never been the only thing. My intuition helped me to connect with people who may not have come from the same place I did. My childhood reminded me to find compassion for their struggles when others simply wanted to warm their hands on the talents of these young stars. My life experiences gave me a way of offering meaningful counsel rather than the tantrums they so often hear in practice and games. My different interests help me give direction without having to relate it to basketball, instead drawing on other things they know or understand or appreciate, whether that's music or movies or business or even dating and relationships.

If I knew only basketball, I could reach a player in only one way; when you have only a hammer, everything looks like a nail. Fortunately, I have more tools stashed away in my garage. A good student can learn anything, while a good teacher can teach anything. Learning and teaching both require being receptive to new ideas.

The Greek philosopher Plato imagined a group of prisoners held captive in a cave since childhood, facing a wall. They can only see the shadows cast on the wall; they don't know about the fire behind them, or the people who walk between the fire and the wall, holding objects whose shadows create the prisoners' only reality. Now imagine that one of them is freed, brought out of the cave into the world, and then returns to try to tell the prisoners about everything he's seen, about the solidity of objects, the light of the fire, the power of the sun. They won't believe him, of course. They will cling to their perceptions. They will find his speculations ridiculous, may label him ignorant, and might turn viciously against him for questioning the validity of the only thing they know.

Large organizations of all kinds resist fundamental change, and the institution of basketball is no different. If you've thought about your world in a particular way all your life, it can be painful to suddenly open yourself to a new perception, a new reality, especially when conveyed by a messenger who doesn't resemble you. But if sports are about excellence, as they claim, and if there are new and better ways of looking at the path to victory, the teams that employ them will be ahead of the game.

In baseball, years of statistics and fresh sources of information have changed the way teams play. Radical defensive shifts are now common, recognizing that some players have pronounced and invariable hitting patterns. Hitters who draw walks are more valued than ever before; pitchers are deployed in shorter stints and greater numbers, mixed and matched, depending on the batter and the situation.

Football teams spread the field, throw the ball with abandon, and gamble on fourth down more and more often. One high school in Arkansas wins state championships by never punting and trying onside kickoffs at nearly every opportunity. These are innovations backed by statistical study and a willingness to let fresh and even radical ideas find their way into the sport.

Basketball's revolution is just beginning to take hold. You can see it in teams that shoot a high number of corner threes, where the arc becomes a straight line and the three-point shot is shorter than it is above the key; it is the highest percentage three-point shot, and it is generally the result of ball movement rather than isolations. Player evaluations based on statistical metrics are growing more sophisticated, making it possible to measure each individual's contribution on both ends of the floor and in relation to the other players on the court at the same time. Training techniques from other realms are increasingly accepted, integrating sophisticated technologies to monitor physiological adaptations or to track movement patterns. The modern world is open in all directions; teams that ignore potential sources of wisdom do so at their peril.

If I work with a player by putting resistance bands around his ankles, or push against his shoulders while he dribbles a ball, or even suggest he try shooting with his eyes closed, it's not because I like to be mysterious; it's because I have something specific in mind, either diagnostic or therapeutic, that may not be obvious to the casual observer. The bands around the ankles are a great tool to help a player with his step-back jumper; they force him to stay on balance, because if he crosses his legs in any way at that moment, he'll trip and fall. If a player thinks there's something off in his release, I might ask him to try closing his eyes to see if the problem is really in his judgment of distance rather than the mechanics of his shot. Pressing against the shoulders of a player while he dribbles, mimicking a football sled, requires him to generate more force than he does when he sprints and jumps, while also making him accustomed to contact as he dribbles. There's always a point, and the more intimately I get to work with a player, the more I can help him; I'll never stop trying to think of new ways to help my guys get better.

It is magical to be out there on the court, working, inventing, engaging, motivating, teaching, and learning. But becoming better, in every capacity, isn't confined to a ninety-four-by-fifty-foot space. So I spend time, lots of time, with them, debating, laughing, talking, finding out more about them from them—because there might be something I can use to help them or something they can teach me, or simply a value in forging a bond based on a game that we love. I have watched so many of the players I have worked with for years evolve as players and people. The evolution is symbolic to me: If they can grow for the better, then so can the sport that brought us together.

We've all heard the expression "Everything works out for the best." Is there any sentiment more exasperating? I can understand the desire to comfort someone who is going through tough times, but where is the comfort in hearing that the thing that's upsetting you is going to prove to be a blessing? "Your feelings are wrong," it says, "and someday you'll see that I'm right."

But I believe forces exist that guide our paths more intelligently than we could do ourselves, and the saying holds more truth than we want to admit at first. I've been very lucky, not just in where I wound up but in how I got here. And by the time I was ready to accept this wisdom, I had reached the point where I no longer needed the comfort. #findyourownway

ACKNOWLEDGMENTS

This book is the culmination of decades of experiences chasing the game. It began as nothing more than a few anecdotes several years ago: As I continued to write, the memories and voices from my childhood, friends, family, and colleagues supported and inspired me, urged me on, and I now extend them my most heartfelt thanks.

To my childhood neighbors Mr. and Mrs. Lemer, thank you for never shooing me away even when I shot baskets on your driveway at dawn. Beyond the Doritos and crumb cakes you always kept in your pantry for post-workout snacks, you recognized early on the magic spell the game had cast on me. My childhood friends Joel Gerwin, Josh Feinberg, Josh Saypol, Josh Kolko, David Sandler, and Paul Nussbaum chipped in to buy me the gift of a lifetime for my bar mitzvah: a hoop my dad fastened to the roof of our garage. Even though it stood nearly eleven feet high as it draped over our driveway, I spent endless hours tossing the ball into the basket. Feinberg, Kolko, and Nussbaum—along with Seth Frey and Jeremy Wohlberg—were among the high school teammates who taught me about friendship, watched the game take hold of me, and gave me my first taste of true camaraderie.

My childhood friend Shelly Finkel embraced my dream, cheered for me when so few did, shed a tear as she watched those

University of Maryland walk-on tryouts from the highest rows of Cole Field House stands, and kept her dorm room refrigerator fully stocked so I could snack after long hours in the gym.

To my best friend, Dr. David Sandler, the greatest heart doctor in the world, who continues to make time—despite all the hours in surgery—to answer every text, take every call, support my endeavors, and attend every NBA All-Star weekend with me to celebrate a journey we could never have imagined.

To Charles Murray, Christian Vazquez, and all the kind people who follow me on Twitter and Facebook, who encouraged me to write and who found inspiration in my messages.

To Carmelo Anthony, Gilbert Arenas, Trevor Ariza, Leandro Barbosa, José Barea, Alana Beard, Steve Blake, Eric Bledsoe, Elton Brand, Kobe Bryant, Matt Carroll, Earl Clark, Stephen Curry, Juan Dixon, Andre Drummond, Jared Dudley, Kevin Durant, Ray Felton, Steve Francis, Rudy Gay, Blake Griffin, James Harden, Brendan Haywood, Grant Hill, Dwight Howard, Ersan Ilyasova, Jarrett Jack, LeBron James, Antawn Jamison, Jonas Jerebko, Joe Johnson, Wes Johnson, Kara Lawson, Ty Lawson, Kevin Love, Roger Mason, Wes Matthews, Ben McLemore, Greg Monroe, Maya Moore, Joakim Noah, Steve Novak, Emeka Okafor, Sasha Pavlović, Chris Paul, Jason Richardson, Iman Shumpert, Chris Smith, Josh Smith, JR Smith, Jerry Stackhouse, Amar'e Stoudemire, Evan Turner, Dwyane Wade, Delonte West, and so many others for trusting me with something so precious. Some of you have become like family to me and many have become good friends. But with all of you, we have shared time alone in the gym, countless meals, heartfelt conversations, and bellyache laughs while forging a bond and chasing a dream.

To Reggie Saunders and the team at Nike Jordan Brand for the amazing opportunity to help bring the game to many deserving young people.

To David Dean, Elena Bergeron, Brian Beletic, Tara Nicolas, Ivan Solotaroff, Ricardo Viramontes, Tina Fryar, and Bettina de Perez, who took time from their extraordinarily busy days to read the roughest of rough drafts and to always comment with honesty.

To Jeff Jacobs at CAA, who would always shuffle his schedule to offer his meaningful counsel when I sought guidance; to Steve Rifkind, whose friendship came with lessons in hustle to help equip me for my newest adventures; and JD Roth, who reinforced that success does not have to trump humility, grace, and gratitude.

David Bauer at *Sports Illustrated* opened his doors and convinced me that the few pages I had written could amount to something, and Thomas LeBien at Simon & Schuster believed I had a story to tell and encouraged me to tell it. I thank them both.

To my literary agent, David Black, and the team at David Black Agency, who challenged me to write with courage, advocated so zealously on my behalf, helped me navigate through unfamiliar terrain, and patiently waited as I matured as a writer.

To my editor Jeff Neuman, who helped weave my anecdotes into a beautiful melody, edited my manuscript with the artistry of a sculptor, and listened to my frustrations with the ear of a friend.

To Charlie Conrad, William Shinker, and the team at Gotham Books for the platform to share my story, as they took a chance on someone who had never written anything beyond some legal memoranda and magazine columns.

To Mairav Mintz and Aynat Ravin, the best sisters a brother could have. Whether it was playing baseball in the yard, building sand castles on Haifa's beaches, eating as many pretzels as we could at our grandmother's house, sharing one can of cola after our swim at the pool, staring from our darkened bedroom window on Halloween night at all the neighborhood kids dressed in their costumes, or quietly praying for me that everything would be OK, your wisdom, care, and compassion always follow and guide me.

To my parents, Dr. Noach and Bracha Ravin, *thank you* doesn't do justice for all you have done. As my life has become filled with more sunshine, it matters to me most to share this warmth with you, whether that means watching you proudly wear all the fantastic Nike gear; serve as my guest of honor at basketball games; introduce you to the guys after the game where they meet you with hugs, hello, and honest concern; quote your wisdom when I am with them; and share with them the lessons of faith and resilience that you taught me. I wouldn't be here if it wasn't for you.

And to the orange ball that keeps my soul alive and my heart bouncing, thank you for rolling into my life.